Red Lobster
The Beginning

RED LOBSTER

The Beginning

CHARLEY WOODSBY

with Chef Dan Drayer

W

WILDERCLIFF PUBLISHING

Text © 2018 Charles E. Woodsby

All rights reserved.

No part of this book may be reproduced or stored in a retrieval system or transmitted in any form or by any means, electronic, mechanical, photocopying, recording, or otherwise, without express written permission of the publisher.

Hardcover ISBN: 978-0-9985369-0-3
Paperback ISBN: 978-0-9985369-1-0
Ebook ISBN: 978-0-9985369-2-7

Library of Congress Control Number: 2018902501

The Red Lobster logo is a trademark of
Red Lobster Hospitality LLC, and is used with permission.

In memory of my first soul mate, Jean.
Thank you for fifty-four wonderful years.

To my second soul mate, my wife, MaryLou.
Thank you for your endless support during the writing of this book.

To God, I give the glory for all my success.

In all thy ways acknowledge Him,
and He shall direct thy paths.

—PROVERBS 3:6 (KJV)

CONTENTS

Acknowledgments		xi
Chapter 1	1931	1
Chapter 2	Values Learned Early	5
Chapter 3	Building a Career	9
Chapter 4	The Thunderbird: A Partnership Is Formed	15
Chapter 5	Old South: Jacksonville's Finest Family Restaurant	19
Chapter 6	Gary's Duck Inn: A Model of Casual Dining	23
Chapter 7	Red Lobster: The Beginning	33
Chapter 8	Hitting It Big	37
Chapter 9	Expansion	41
Chapter 10	An Amazing Time	47
Chapter 11	The Rise of Red Lobster and My Retirement	53
Chapter 12	The Red Lobster Legacy	57
Chapter 13	Every Step of the Way	61
Restaurants		65
Awards		111
Woodsby Family Memories		123
Recipes		135
A Note from the Authors		183
Additional Praise		187

ACKNOWLEDGMENTS

Running this business isn't about me. It is about all the great people who helped to grow the business and make it successful—remarkable people like Bill Darden, Wally Buckley, Joe Lee, Mack Miller, Jim Doherty, Bonnie Lynch, and the many others who contributed to the success of Red Lobster in the early days. In the later years, my own children benefited from this journey I started so long ago, as well as my grandchildren.

I want to acknowledge my son, Ron, for taking over all aspects of the restaurants' operations, which allowed me the freedom to semiretire. His keen vision and creativity have led to the success of the Talk of the Town restaurants.

I want to acknowledge Dennis Darmoc, CFO, and Jackie Hampton, office manager, who have both been with us through the ups and downs for over thirty years, along with countless other employees who have worked so tirelessly to make Talk of the Town everything it is expected to be.

I also want to thank MaryLou (my wife), Juli Drayer, Sherri Darmoc, and Brittanie Olavarria for their countless hours editing this book.

I would like to recognize the next generation of the Talk of the Town Restaurant Group: Clark Woodsby (my grandson), Seth Miller, and Paul Darmoc. I wish them luck as they assist Ron and take the company I am so proud of into the future.

Lastly, grateful appreciation is given to Chef Dan Drayer. It was Chef Dan who came to me with the idea of writing a book about my life in the restaurant business and the actual history of Red Lobster. His inspiration has allowed me to tell my story and share it with the world, especially with the hardworking restaurant employees everywhere who might have a dream and the passion to excel.

1

1931

RECIPE FOR LIFE

I thank God every day that I was born in America, the land of opportunity.

The citizens of Spartanburg, South Carolina, prided themselves on their southern hospitality. Even in the midst of the Great Depression in 1931, families gathered around their dinner tables every evening for supper. Guests were always welcome, even if the fare was simple.

Times were tough in 1931, but you could take in a Saturday matinee at the Montgomery Theatre downtown for twenty-five cents. *Dracula*, a 1931 American horror film starring Bela Lugosi as the title character, was scaring audiences in Spartanburg and across the nation. *The Public Enemy* was released that same year and launched James Cagney to stardom. The Montgomery was packed as audiences sat riveted by the urban crime drama of a young man's rise in the criminal underworld in Prohibition-era America. The movie also featured the beautiful young actress Jean Harlow.

Citizens of Spartanburg could follow the news by reading the *Spartanburg Herald* in the morning and the *Spartanburg Journal* in the evening. On May 31, they would have read that, with the press of a ceremonial button in Washington, DC, President Herbert Hoover turned on the lights of the Empire State Building, located at the corner of Fifth Avenue and Thirty-Fourth Street in New York City. This event officially opened the world's tallest building. Unfortunately, as a result of the Depression, much of the office space in the building's 102 stories remained empty.

On that same day, the headlines reported that the Yangtze River in China peaked during a flood that killed 3.7 million people directly and indirectly over the next several months. The 1931 central China floods were a series of floods that occurred during the Nanjing decade of the Republic of China era. Collectively, these floods are considered the worst natural disaster of the twentieth century and perhaps the deadliest natural disaster ever recorded.

The men of Spartanburg would have followed the 1931 World Series, with the Saint Louis Cardinals beating the Philadelphia Athletics in seven games, a rematch and reversal of fortunes from the 1930 World Series. The spitball pitch was banned by Major League Baseball in 1920, but those who were grandfathered in were permitted to keep it in their arsenals. One of those pitching who still "wet his pill" was Burleigh Grimes, who had two starts, two wins, and seven innings of no-hit pitching in game three.

On June 16, 1931, the *Spartanburg Herald* and *Journal* readers learned that Al Capone had pled guilty to tax evasion and Prohibition charges; he boasted to the press that he had struck a deal for a two-and-a-half-year sentence. But the presiding judge informed him that he, the judge, was not bound by any deal, so Capone changed his plea to not guilty. On October 18, 1931, Capone was convicted after trial and, on November 24, sentenced to eleven years in federal prison.

The fourth Academy Awards ceremony was held on Tuesday, November 10, 1931, at the Sala d'Oro of the Biltmore Hotel. The next morning in Spartanburg, the *Herald* reported that US vice president Charles Curtis attended the banquet and was one of the

event's several speakers. Trying to stay up a little too late, ten-year-old Jackie Cooper, nominated for Best Actor, fell asleep during the ceremony.

In 1931, construction began on the Hoover Dam, standing today as a concrete arch-gravity dam in the Black Canyon of the Colorado River on the border of Arizona and Nevada. Its construction, continuing until 1936, entailed a massive effort involving thousands of workers and costing over a hundred lives. President Franklin Roosevelt dedicated the dam on September 30, 1935. In its planning stages, it was known as Boulder Dam. The Herbert Hoover administration changed the name to Hoover Dam in 1930 as a political move, but in 1933, the Roosevelt administration changed it back to Boulder Dam. Then, under Harry Truman, the name of Hoover Dam was restored, and the name became permanent.

The citizens of Spartanburg likely didn't hear about Gerald Ford, who, while attending the University of Michigan, played center on the football team, earning three varsity letters and being named Most Valuable Player on the 1934 squad. The year 1931 saw him playing in both the East-West Shrine Game and the College All-Star Game. Ford received professional football contract offers from the Green Bay Packers and the Detroit Lions, both of which he declined.

But everyone heard that Amelia Earhart married George Putnam. There was no honeymoon for the newlyweds, as Amelia was involved in a nine-day cross-country tour promoting auto gyros for the tour sponsor, Beech-Nut Gum.

At the same time, Ronald Reagan won an award for his performance in *Aria da Capo*, part of a collegiate drama competition sponsored by Northwestern University.

Oh, and one more thing happened in the year 1931. Careful readers of the *Herald* or *Journal* might have caught a birth announcement. A boy was born to William Dan and Lucy Marie Woodsby. They named him Charles Edward Woodsby. But everyone would call me Charley.

RECIPE FOR LIFE

Theodore Roosevelt stated that the best manager is the one who has sense enough to pick good men to do what you want done and the self-restraint enough to keep from meddling with them while they do it. Turn them loose; let them go.

2

Values Learned Early

RECIPE FOR LIFE

Service, service, service. We are in the service business; pay attention to the details.

We were a family of nine. My older siblings were Grace, Frank, and Amos. Those younger were Betty, Bill, and Peggy. I was right smack in the middle. Up until I was ten, we lived on a farm, and my parents worked at Drayton Cotton Mill in Spartanburg. My father earned fifty cents a day.

Our home was a simple three-bedroom house, and I mean simple. This was the Depression. Our "bathroom" was an outhouse that we were able to procure through the Works Projects Administration, a large federal relief agency that was part of Franklin Delano Roosevelt's New Deal policy. Yes, the WPA provided major public projects, but they provided some minor private services too, including outhouses, believe it or not. The outhouse came complete with a cement floor and a vent pipe. There was no window, but it did provide some privacy and protection from the rain. One- and two-holers were available from the WPA, and because we had a large family, we were lucky enough to get a two-holer. And it wasn't just us in that three-bedroom house, either. We often had relatives living with us who couldn't find work.

At the age of eight, I milked cows before school and helped pick cotton. One of our cows was bitten by a rabid dog one time. Her behavior became very strange. We put her in a stall in the barn, and she just kept walking in circles. Meanwhile, the whole family had been drinking the milk that came from this cow, and we all had to get vaccines—shots! One a day for twenty-one days. The cow, of course, had to be put down and buried so the rabies wouldn't spread to other animals.

During the winter my brothers and I operated rabbit traps. When we caught the rabbits, our job was to kill and skin them. We were a poor family, and everyone was expected to contribute. At the age of nine, I picked blackberries and sold them for ten cents a gallon. I had to save up for my school overalls, which cost seventy-five cents and which I was expected to pay for.

We drew water from a well and canned our own food. We had our own apple trees and canned our apples. Canning was popular at that time because there was no refrigeration. We raised our own hogs, chickens, and beef. We grew our own vegetables too. During the summer, we would load our vegetables into my father's truck and sell door to door to the neighbors. The only things we bought from the local grocery store were sugar, flour, and coffee. If a grocery order was five dollars or more, we received a complimentary candy bar or pack of gum. That was a real treat for us kids.

When we finally got electricity, each room of the house had a single light bulb hanging from the center of the ceiling. There were no light fixtures at that time, so we kids had to do our studies under that single bulb.

In 1941, when I was ten, my father sold the farm for $5,000, and we moved closer to my parents' workplace. Around that time, my older sister, Grace, left the nest to work at a war plant in Paterson, New Jersey. Frank left for Huntington Station, Long Island, New York, to work at our uncle Roy's restaurant, Cozy Corner. Amos joined the military. We were now a family of six living in a two-bedroom house. We had a kitchen, a sitting room with a fireplace, and two bedrooms. We now had running water as well as a government-issued two-holer outhouse.

I attended the Whitney School in Spartanburg. To and from school, I had to walk one and a quarter miles each way down the railroad tracks. My shoes wore out, and my parents slid cardboard inside them to serve as soles. No way we could afford to have shoes resoled back then. New shoes? Out of the question.

At eleven, I was given my first job outside the house. I worked at Rash's, the local grocery store, part time during the week and all day on Saturday. I waited on customers and filled and delivered orders. At that time chicken and cow feed were offered in the grocery store, and we would deliver orders door to door to customers' houses. My pay was fifty cents a day during the week and one dollar on Saturday.

Life at home was hard. As I grew older, I began to consider that maybe I could make a better life for myself. But how? Seems like for guys back in those days from poor families like mine, there was at least one strong possibility for moving ahead in life. I began thinking hard about joining the service.

VALUES LEARNED EARLY

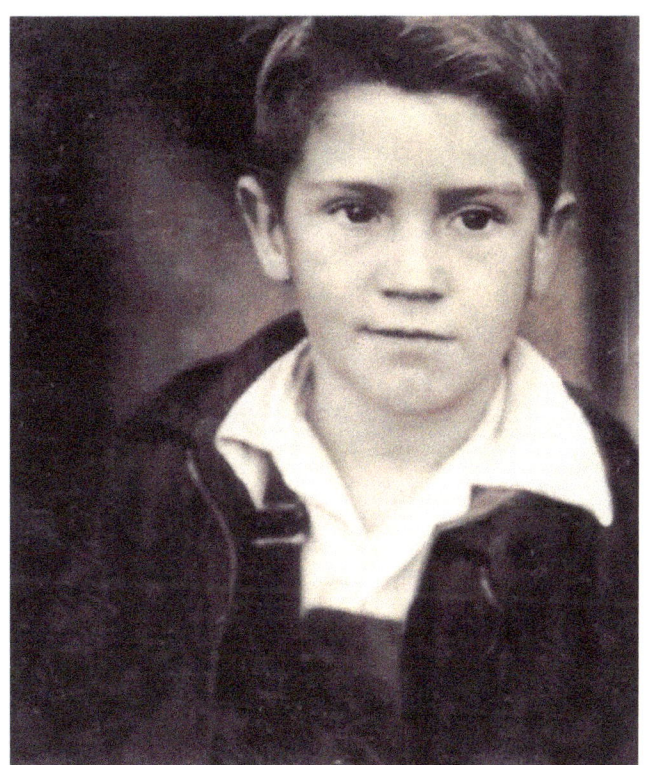

Me at eight years old

1930s WPA public outhouse

Drayton Mills, Spartanburg, South Carolina

RED LOBSTER...THE BEGINNING

Me at eleven years old

Our home in 1941, Spartanburg, South Carolina

Rash's grocery store in the 1940s

Whitney Elementary School, Spartanburg, South Carolina

RECIPE FOR LIFE

My motto has always been quality, value, service, and integrity; be honest, be truthful, and treat people with respect.

3

Building a Career

RECIPE FOR LIFE

The law of sacrifice: you can't move upward without giving something up. Be ready to pay a price.

In 1946, I registered for the military draft. The only problem was that I was just fifteen years old. But I claimed to be eighteen, and in October of that year, I enlisted with the US Air Force. My basic training was at Sack Field Air Force Base in San Antonio, Texas, and from there, I was sent overseas to Tachikawa Air Force Base in Yokohama, Japan. Then I was assigned to Kimpo Air Force Base in South Korea. After being accepted to radio and radar school, I was reassigned to Japan to attend Keio University for a sixteen-week training course in radio and radar. After I finished my coursework, it was back to Korea.

In Korea, I was a radio operator on C-46 and C-47 cargo planes, and we flew supplies into different parts of the country. The planes had been vital to the success of many Allied campaigns— in particular, those at Guadalcanal,

Tachikawa Air Force Base, Japan, main gate

Me and the boys

where the plane made it possible for Allied troops to counter the mobility of the light-traveling Japanese army. The C-46 was the largest and heaviest twin-engine aircraft in the air corps. Its huge cargo capacity (twice that of the C-47), large cargo doors, powerful engines, and long range made it ideal for vast distances. The advantage of the C-47 was that it was lighter and could take off and land using a much shorter runway. Those planes were so reliable, they said you could tie them together with baling wire.

When I came back from Korea and Japan in 1948, I ended up in Smyrna, Tennessee, as a radio operator doing endurance testing on a Flying Boxcar, a flying 182. Our other duties were to drop paratroopers at Fort Campbell in Kentucky and Fort Benning in Georgia. It seemed we were on the ground only long enough to service the plane.

In October 1949, I officially left the air force as a sergeant. After I returned home to Spartanburg, South Carolina, the recruiting officer came out to visit repeatedly, trying to get me to reenlist, but it was just not in my heart to do so.

I considered going to the RCA school to be trained as a field rep for repairs and maintenance of equipment and to sell and assist with the correct use of RCA's equipment in the military. Owing to the amount of money the military was spending on developing defense technologies at the time, this could have been huge.

Instead, I enrolled in Cecil Business College to learn basic business principles. And in 1950, I attended interior design school in High Point, North Carolina, a four-week course where I learned about matching colors, correcting furnishing asymmetries, and room decorating.

That same year, I spotted a beautiful young lady at a local five-and-ten store. I admired her

Leaving the service

Jean Harris and me, 1950

Jean and me, 1951

from afar but didn't get the chance to meet her. Still, I couldn't seem to stop thinking about her. A couple of weeks later, I saw her again, this time at a dance I was attending on a double date with a buddy of mine, Bill Bagwell. I drove my date home, probably faster than I should have, and returned to the dance only to discover that the young lady had already left. But as it turned out, Bill's date was a friend of the young lady's, and Bill was able to make arrangements for me to meet her the next day. Her name was Jean Harris, and I knew from the beginning that she was the one for me. In 1951, Jean and I were married at my sister's home in Spartanburg, South Carolina.

In 1951, I went to work in the furniture business, decorating windows and rooms, making $45 per week. Jean worked in a shirt factory, making $25 per week. My brother Frank, on the other hand, was working at a diner in New York City and making $116 per

Wedding day in Spartanburg, South Carolina: a double ceremony—Faye and Bill Bagwell with Jean and me

RED LOBSTER...THE BEGINNING

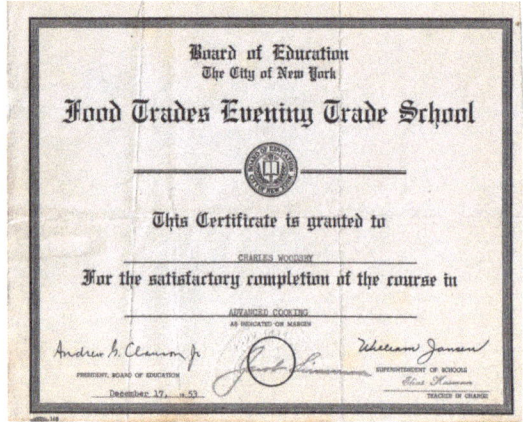

My advanced cooking diploma

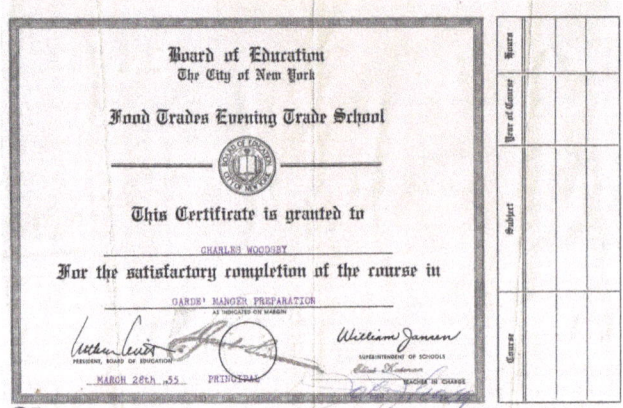

My garde manger certificate

week. Jean and I realized that's where we needed to be. And so we went to New York to find our future.

I took a job in the diner and started taking culinary classes at night. Jean got a job as a waitress at the Brass Rail, a higher-end restaurant specializing in huge lunchtime deli sandwiches, complete with a carver in the window. The Brass Rail also had a restaurant on Jones Beach in Long Island, and it was something of a landmark. It had opened in 1929 by then governor Franklin D. Roosevelt just months after the Wall Street crash that had led to the Great Depression.

In September of 1952, Jean and I were blessed with a baby boy. We named him Ronnie Edward. Jean's widowed mother moved to New York City to care for little Ronnie while Jean was at work.

In 1952, I went to work in a sandwich shop in Union Square, Manhattan, where I joined the union. I went through both chef and management training. I was beginning to make a career for myself in the restaurant business.

From 1952 to 1955, I studied at the Hotel and Restaurant Management School and Culinary School in New York City with classically trained Swiss chefs and teachers. It was quite an education for me. We learned everything about the aging, butchering, and grades of beef and all about fresh seafood,

Some typical butcher-store prices of the era

12

BUILDING A CAREER

With Jean in our New York apartment

as well as traditional basics, like soups and stocks. There were classes in garde manger, baking, and all the stations of the professional kitchen. The popular dishes of the time were oxtail ragout, beef tips, Salisbury steak, stuffed cabbage, and sole.

In 1955, Jean and I decided to move out of New York. We wanted to raise our family in a smaller city—but one that was still large enough for good business opportunities. We went south, to Atlanta, Georgia, taking our life savings of $14,000 with us. With that, we purchased a restaurant called the Rose Bowl Tea Room, renaming it the 17th Street Tea Room. The location was where the two Peach Tree streets met at Persian Point. The Tea Room was beautiful, with an evening service that seemed to exceed everybody's expectations.

Meanwhile, I noticed a lot of the older property of Atlanta, even mansions, being purchased and turned into high-rise office buildings. To serve the new businesses, I started opening the Tea Room for lunch service, and breakfast service soon followed. The restaurant was so successful that I sold it, thinking that I could replicate my success on a much larger scale.

In 1956, I opened a restaurant called Persian Point. I leased the building and completely renovated it. But I invested too much money in the equipment and renovations and didn't have enough operating capital to make the payments. This was a great lesson in managing money. I had overextended myself. My business model had failure built

Heading to Atlanta

Peach Tree Street in Atlanta, Georgia, 1956

into it. In time, the restaurant might have done very well, but I didn't have enough money to survive the time needed to get there. It was the most humbling experience of my professional career.

By necessity, I got out of Persian Point and, in fact, almost got out of the restaurant business. By 1957, our family was growing. Ronnie found himself with a little sister that year when Deborah Marie was born, and in 1958, along came another baby girl, Sherry Lynn. I had a family to support, and any dreams I had of being a successful restaurateur were put on hold indefinitely. I took a job delivering milk for Miss Georgia Dairies, and I committed to being the best I could be. I rose at three o'clock every morning and made my deliveries by ten, spending the rest of the morning knocking on doors to find new customers. The company had an incentive program; we'd get a bonus for each new customer we brought on board. I built up my route so well that they offered me a supervisory position. Now I had a choice to make: stay in the dairy business or get back in the restaurant business.

Jean made the choice easy. "Your love is the restaurant business," she told me. "That's where you need to be." Jean, of course, was right, and with her support, I left Miss Georgia Dairies and took a job working at a Davis Brothers Cafeteria. I was back where I belonged.

RECIPE FOR LIFE

A natural passion in any business creates a relentless pursuit that allows for true inspiration for development of the passion in others.

4

The Thunderbird: A Partnership Is Formed

RECIPE FOR LIFE

*Always do more than what is expected of you.
Go the extra mile. Keep your heart and soul in the business.*

At a Georgia Restaurant Association meeting, I was introduced to Bill Darden. Bill was the president of the association and had a large restaurant portfolio, including a major part of the franchises of Howard Johnson. In addition to his Howard Johnson franchises, he was running the Green Frog, Bonanza, and Kentucky Fried Chicken operations in the area.

Bill's restaurant career started early. He opened his first restaurant—the Green Frog—when he was just nineteen. It was in the late 1930s in Waycross, Georgia, and the place was a twenty-five-seat Depression-era drive-in. With the slogan "Service with a Hop," the Green Frog was a big hit and a local landmark. Bill was a real southern gentleman. As

an industry publication once put it, "With a twang resonant of Southern aristocracy, a distinguished mane of white hair and a button-down, gentlemanly persona, William B. Darden appeared more like a studio extra from *Gone with the Wind* than a restaurateur."[1]

As it turned out, Bill was looking for a new manager for a restaurant of his in Jacksonville named the Thunderbird. The Thunderbird was leased from and adjacent to a hotel of the same name, owned by the Stein family. The restaurant was losing money. I was still with Davis Brothers Cafeteria, but I was getting fed up with working for someone else. I wanted to go into business for myself again, and Bill and I began discussing the possibility of a partnership at the Thunderbird. The discussion continued over time, with me ultimately telling Bill and his brother Denim (also known as D. C.), with whom Bill owned the Thunderbird, that I wanted the chance to come in and turn the place around. If successful, I'd be allowed a one-third share of the restaurant at book value with a portion of the increase in profits going toward my share. Bill and Denim agreed. They'd pay me $600 a month base, 10 percent of the first $10,000 profit, 15 percent of the next $15,000, and 20 percent thereafter.

In 1960, Jean and I moved the family to Jacksonville, and I started working on my end of the bargain. The Thunderbird had a lot of potential, but it was hemorrhaging money. I knew I needed to make some drastic alterations. I started with the menu, completely changing it. We started cooking from scratch and training the employees to focus on putting out great flavor and quality. When I arrived at the restaurant, it only seated 260. We remodeled the main dining room and called it the King's Hearth Steakhouse. It had exhibition cooking with an open pit. We started focusing on putting out fresh, quality food with great flavor and training our employees to exemplify professional standards.

We had no liquor license, though. A restaurant at that time had to get an existing retail or package liquor license to serve alcohol, and at the time there were none available. And so we got creative. Jax's Liquors was right next door to the Thunderbird and was owned and operated by Don Trednick. Jax's not only was a liquor store but also had a lounge with 175 seats. We decided to expand the restaurant, adding 100 seats for a supper club and a 400-seat banquet room, which could be divided into three separate rooms. We combined the lounge at Jax's with the new supper club and called it the Mayan Room, hiring a chef out of Chicago named Chef Pierson. It was a huge hit. We had entertainment in the lounge that was on par with shows in Las Vegas. Quite a few of the popular 1950s and early-1960s groups played there.

One of our more popular banquet items was our Chicken Italiano. At a restaurant show, I'd met a gentleman named S. Truett Cathy, who sold these beautiful, marinated four-ounce chicken breasts. We started ordering them. I would fry the breast and top it with marinara sauce and Parmesan cheese and serve it over spaghetti. This dish became

---

1   Bill Carlino, "William Darden," *Nation's Restaurant News*, February 1996.

one of our most inexpensive items to make. You may have heard of Truett. Eventually, he took those seasoned chicken breasts and started Chick-fil-A.

The Thunderbird began to flourish. In addition to my stake in the business, Bill Darden rewarded my skills in other ways. Soon I was supervising not only the Thunderbird but also two Howard Johnsons. I was also a partner in the Green Frog in Adel, Georgia.

Original Thunderbird wait staff

Thunderbird Inn, Jacksonville, Florida

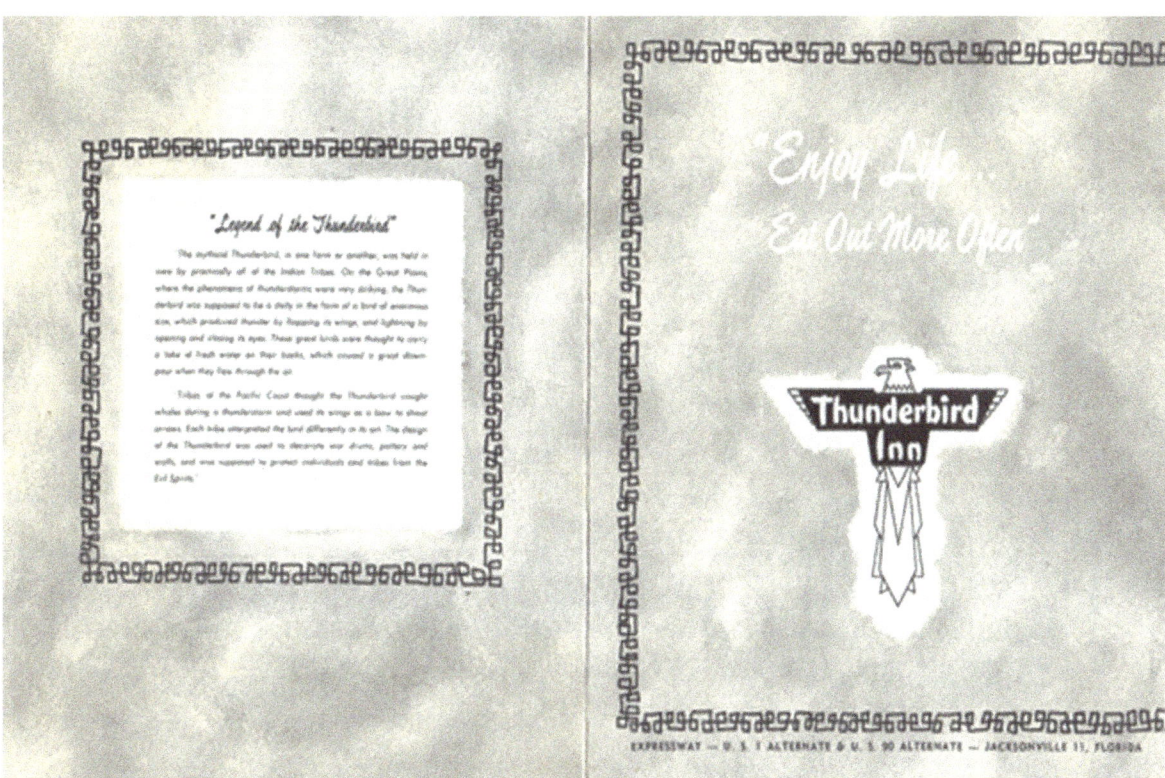
Original Thunderbird Inn brochure

Original Thunderbird Inn menu

With Chef Pierson at the Thunderbird

RECIPE FOR LIFE

Do it now. Whatever it is, think it, act it, and live it.

5

Old South: Jacksonville's Finest Family Restaurant

RECIPE FOR LIFE

We have to continue to guide, train, and train. Critique and help our people to improve their performance in every way, every day, and give them praise for a job well done. Build confidence and a sense of belonging—keep our people motivated and positive!

In Jacksonville, in 1961, I met the owner of the Old South restaurant. He was an older gentleman, maybe around seventy, and he'd come into the Thunderbird nearly every afternoon and sit down and have a cup of coffee. I got to talking with him, and soon enough we became friends. His restaurant was just as the name implied: Old South. Biscuits and honey, all fresh vegetables, and everything made from scratch.

As it turned out, he was getting ready to retire. He had no family—no kids to leave his restaurant to—and he suggested that

In Jacksonville, 1963

maybe I should take over his business. I was intrigued. It was a decent place with a good following, but I suspected I could make it more profitable than it was. It had an old-style 1950s-type decor, with Formica-top dinette tables. It definitely needed some updating. We settled on a one-year lease with an option to buy. After one year, I bought it and then started remodeling.

With my first-year profits and a bank loan, I remodeled the front of the restaurant. I put in beautiful brick flooring, a sign on the other side of the building, a mural of an antebellum scene across the walls, and comfortable captain's chairs. After the second year, I updated the kitchen. Business improved significantly, and we had to add a walk-in cooler to store the food.

I marketed the restaurant pretty heavily too, especially around the immediate area. I was still working at the Thunderbird, typically until after one in the morning, the closing time for the supper club. I'd get a few hours of sleep and then rise early to put menus under the windshield wipers of all the cars around the neighborhoods adjacent to the Old South. It paid off. The third and fourth years saw even more growth. We were breaking $100,000 annually, a lot of money back in those days, especially for a one-hundred-seat restaurant.

The Old South was a real family affair. Jean worked there often, relieving the managers on their off days. Sometimes she couldn't find a babysitter for the girls, and she'd bring them in with her. They'd help out too; I can still picture them sitting in the kitchen snapping green beans. Ron was fifteen by then and started out washing dishes. The girls would never have food service aspirations (Deborah would go on to become a successful Realtor and Sherry a skilled teacher), but Ron was headed for the restaurant business right from the start. He learned it from the ground up back in those Old South days. From dishwasher, he'd go on to work every position in that restaurant.

For me, the Old South provided a lifelong lesson: hard work pays off. I gave it my all, and the Old South reciprocated with a steady flow of happy customers and a terrific bottom line.

Once I had things running smoothly, I advertised for a manager for the Old South, and Maude Davis showed up to apply for the job. She had worked for Gary Starling, owner of Gary's Duck Inn in Orlando. I ended up hiring her. Soon I'd get to know Gary. His Gary's Duck Inn, a simple place with great food, would ultimately provide the blueprint for a restaurant empire.

OLD SOUTH: JACKSONVILLE'S FINEST FAMILY RESTAURANT

With the staff at the Old South during Christmas

Staff at the Old South

Old South
Jacksonville's Finest Family Restaurant

DINNER MENU

Boiled Spare Ribs with Rice	$1.65
Beef Stew with Fresh Vegetables	$1.65
Fried Chicken Feast W/French Fries	$1.55
One Fourth Baked Chicken W/Dressing	$1.60
Broiled Hamburger Steak, Au Jus	$1.75
Grilled Genuine Calves Liver, Bacon Strip	$1.85
Breaded Milk Fed Veal Cutlet W/Tomato Sauce	$1.75
Combination Plate - Fried Jumbo Shrimp & Scallops, Tartar Sauce	$1.90
Grilled Deviled Crab Meat Pattie	$1.65
Fried Deep Sea Trout W/Tartar Sauce	$1.85
Fried Fantail Shrimp W/French Fries	$1.95
Broiled Spanish Mackerel	$1.75
Fried Select Oysters W/French Fries	$1.90
Fresh Whole Flounder, Broiled or Fried	$1.95
Fried Deep Sea Scallops W/French Fries	$1.80
Grilled Western Pork Chops	$1.85
Baked Sugar Cured Ham W/Pineapple Ring	$1.75

Choice of Two Garden Fresh Vegetables, Tea or Coffee, Dessert

Fresh Turnips & Greens	Carrot & Raisin Salad
Fresh Yellow Squash	Tossed Green Salad
Steamed Rice & Gravy	Fresh Cottage Cheese
Fresh String Beans	Creamy Cole Slaw
Baked Macaroni & Cheese	Spiced Pickled Beets
Hot Buttered Apples	Sliced Home Grown Tomatoes
Mashed Potatoes	Apple Sauce

RECIPE FOR LIFE

*If you have a problem, get on top of it right away.
The longer you put it off, the worse it will become!*

6

Gary's Duck Inn: A Model of Casual Dining

RECIPE FOR LIFE

Just because we are doing something one way doesn't mean we should keep doing it that way. Keep on top of it; there could be a better way.

Gary Starling had a summer home in Tryon, North Carolina. When he would come through Jacksonville on his way back to his place in Orlando, he'd stop and visit Maude Davis. He and I got to know each other and over time became great friends. Gary talked of his Gary's Duck Inn, and I showed him all through the Thunderbird. In 1963, on the way back from vacationing in Clearwater, Jean and I stopped in Orlando and had lunch at Gary's restaurant. It was right on Orange Blossom Trail, and we liked it. Several months later, while I was out on the road, Maude Davis contacted me to see whether I might be interested in a restaurant with a yearly revenue of $500,000. In 1963 this was considered a high-volume restaurant. Gary was having some health problems and was interested in selling the business. He had told Maude that he wanted me to have it.

GARY'S DUCK INN
1962-1994

23

Gary's Duck Inn, "Where good food predominates," had catered to the growing number of locals and increasing influx of tourists since it had opened in 1944. The restaurant had had humble beginnings. Gary and Caroline Starling originally had three employees and seating for fifteen patrons; it was basically a bar in an old house. They served fried shrimp, French fries, coleslaw, and hush puppies. Gary frequently ran to the local grocery stores for supplies, and local fishermen dropped by with their catches.

In the beginning the restaurant and kitchen were run by Maude, who was one of just three employees. By 1957 the number of employees had grown to fifty-five. Bonnie Lynch was hired in the mid-1960s as a cashier and was promoted to dining room manager. The food was being delivered by as many as ten trucks per day.

During lobster season, customers consumed eighty-five thousand pounds of the Florida delicacy, as reported in a major article in the local *Florida Sentinel*. But the image Gary used most often to whet customers' appetites was the gargantuan ring of fried shrimp with homemade cocktail sauce in the center. Every day Gary would have a picture in the newspaper of the huge shrimp platter floating over the restaurant. The popularity was magnetic and drew celebrities, locals, and tourists from far and wide to feast on the freshly breaded crispy fried shrimp during season.

Even the famous Duncan Hines loved Gary's Duck Inn and listed it in his 1954 guidebook, *Adventures in Good Eating: A Guidebook to the Best Restaurants along America's Highways*. Besides the famous shrimp platter, the Duncan Hines guidebook also mentioned another of Gary's dishes: hush puppies, those little cornmeal bundles of fried delight. Marjorie Kinnan Rawlings, the famous Florida writer, declared hush puppies "in a class by themselves: Fresh caught fried fish without hush puppies are man without woman, a beautiful woman without kindness, law without policemen." She also provided some history. The name supposedly derived from hunting dogs incessantly howling for the food they smelled during hunting and fishing expeditions. "Cooks or sportsmen tossed the remaining cornmeal patties to the dogs, calling, 'Hush, puppies!' and the dogs, devouring them, could ask no more of life, and hushed."[2] Duncan Hines could say about them only, "Yum—Yum."[3]

Needless to say, I was very interested in Gary's Duck Inn. I got a hold of Bill Darden, and we both met with Gary. We were ready to sign a deal for the local landmark restaurant.

---

[2] Marjorie Kinnan Rawlings, *Cross Creek Cookery* (New York: C. Scribner's Sons, 1942), 28.

[3] Dickinson, *Orlando*, 139–40. See also Dorothy Chapman, "Gary's Duck Inn Fried Shrimp," *Orlando Sentinel*, February 13, 1986; "Mousse Pie from Gary's Duck Inn," *Orlando Sentinel*, March 29, 1990; "Gator Tail with Swamp Sauce Appetizer from Gary's Duck Inn," *Orlando Sentinel*, April 25, 1991; "Gary's Duck Inn Is Gone but Seafood Bisque Lives On," *Orlando Sentinel*, November 10, 1994; and Dorothy Chapman and Heather J. McPherson, *Another Taste of Florida: The Best of Thought You'd Never Ask* (New York: McGraw-Hill, 1993). See also Joy Wallace Dickinson, "Looking Back on Culinary Hot Spots in Central Florida," *Orlando Sentinel*, August 8, 2010.

GARY'S DUCK INN: A MODEL OF CASUAL DINING

I remember that Gary started to celebrate the relationship a little early, and Bill and I ended up having to help him to the table. Bill and I brought Bill's brother D. C. in as a partner, along with Al Woods. Al had worked as a manager for a Howard Johnson's in Charleston, South Carolina, and was ready to make a change. For my part, I had to cash in a life insurance policy to cover my percent of the deal.

After the purchase, Al Woods and Wally Buckley managed the place. Wally was a charismatic promoter originally from Chicago whose restaurant in Clearwater had been destroyed by a hurricane. Unfortunately, he hadn't had hurricane insurance. He found us from an ad I'd run for a manager. I hired him, and he trained at the Thunderbird and then took the position at Gary's. From the start, Wally had a bigger picture in mind, a picture of expansion and growth.

The 160 seats grew to 325 seats, but the restaurant continued to be known for great fresh, local, no-frills seafood that featured quality, service, and affordable pricing. Its continued popularity drew huge numbers of fans from miles around. Entertainers Bob Hope and Dolly Parton, baseball great Rod Carew, and basketball star Daryl Dawkins[4] ate many of the two thousand pounds of shrimp served per week each year during the restaurant's 1970s and 1980s heyday.

I knew shrimp season was coming when the white shrimp would begin running north of Saint Mary's, Georgia, migrating south along the coast of Florida, and going back out to the sea south of Cape Canaveral. All the local fishermen would show up at the back door to sell their catches. They'd bring fish to us or Vince Lombardi, a local restaurant purveyor of seafood, but they always came to us first. We also bought large quantities of shrimp and then froze them.

One food review, from Chris Sherman of the *Orlando Sentinel*, read, "There's no salmon here, but there is flounder, grouper, tilefish, snapper, frogs' legs, clams, oysters, crab legs and some alligator—an inventory that would seem to require long-established supply lines."[5]

Shortly after I discovered Gary's, a California businessman named Walter Elias Disney flew over Orlando in a private plane and took note of how the intersection of newly constructed I-4 and the Florida Turnpike would bring people together from all over the East Coast. He also noticed the abundance of undeveloped land all around that intersection. By 1965 Walt Disney had used shell corporations to buy 27,258 acres, and he announced his plans to create "the greatest attraction yet known in the history of Florida."

---

[4] Christine Shenot and Kevin Spears, "Orlando Landmark Fades Away: Gary's Duck Inn, an Orlando Landmark and the Inspiration behind the Red Lobster Seafood Closed Last Week. It Was 49," *Orlando Sentinel*, October 11, 1994.

[5] Chris Sherman, "Seafood Pure and Plentiful," *Orlando Sentinel*, June 2, 1985.

Walt would not live to see his Disney World completed; tragically, he died of lung cancer the following year, at age sixty-five. But his boasting did not prove empty. In 1969, only 3.5 million tourists visited Orlando. In its first year, 1971, Disney World alone had 10.7 million visitors, drawing people to Central Florida from all over America. Over the next decade, the explosion of new tourist attractions, the era of cheap gas, and the increasing use of air conditioning—both in cars and in buildings—drew more and more people to the state. Here they discovered the regional specialty: great seafood. Soon, a restaurant inspired by Gary's would bring great seafood to them.[6]

Gary's Duck Inn, "The American Family Seafood Restaurant." In 1949 air conditioning was added in the dining room on the north side and in a small private dining room. The kitchen space tripled, and parking increased to four times the original size.

Photo taken in 1954

By 1955, Gary Starling had a $500,000-a-year restaurant operation.

---

[6] Tracy J. Revels, *Sunshine Paradise: A History of Florida Tourism* (Gainesville: University Press of Florida, 2011), 120–24.

GARY'S DUCK INN: A MODEL OF CASUAL DINING

In 1959, Gary's was completely remodeled.

Last remodel, 1981; view after South Orange Blossom Trail was widened, eliminating the entire front parking lot.

Cover of new menu after 1981 remodeling

RED LOBSTER...THE BEGINNING

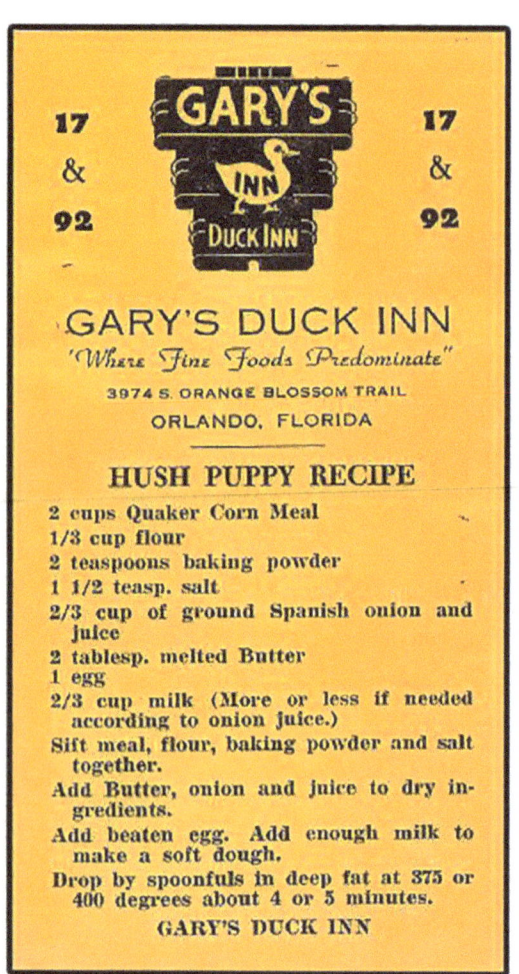 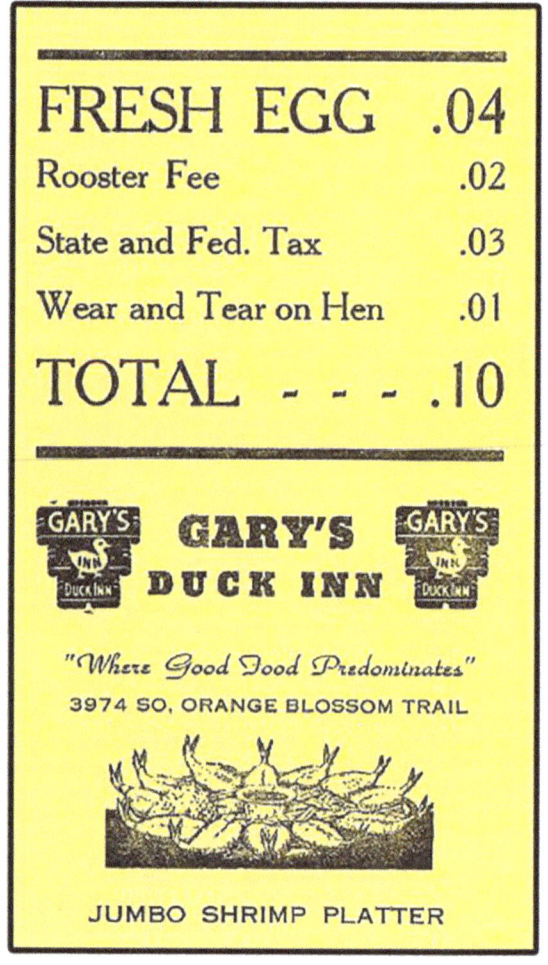

The recipe for Gary's hush puppies was requested so much, cards were eventually printed and handed out. (The backside of the card reveals Gary's sense of humor.)

GARY'S DUCK INN: A MODEL OF CASUAL DINING

The family at Gary's: Ron, Debbie, me, Sherry, and Jean

Gary's Duck Inn famous fried-shrimp dinner

Gary's Duck Inn fried-chicken dinner

Gary's Duck Inn trout dinner

Gary's Duck Inn Florida grouper dinner

RED LOBSTER...THE BEGINNING

Gary's Duck Inn

Gary's Duck Inn wait staff (Gary Starling, far right)

GARY'S DUCK INN
Yesterday and Today

In 1945, Gary Starling opened for business with a seating capacity of 30 people and a staff of three persons. Back in these beginning days, the motto was: "Duck in . . . Waddle Out."

In 1963, Al Woods, Bill Darden, Charlie Woodsby and Denham Darden began operating Gary's and started expanding it to the size it is today. They honored the tradition of the original Gary's and were careful to retain the friendly, informal atmosphere and the superb quality of the food.

Gary's really thinks that you are someone special. We thank you for dining with us and we look forward to seeing you again and again. After all, if you eat at Gary's once, you'll be back!

Gary's Duck Inn 1945

Gary's Duck Inn 1954

Gary's Duck Inn 1959

Gary's Duck Inn 1981

RED LOBSTER...THE BEGINNING

Jean and me with Julie Woods and a guest at Gary's Duck Inn

Bill and Mary Darden with Jean and me at Gary's Duck Inn

RECIPE FOR LIFE

Find your passion for what you really want to do in life—schoolteacher, boat captain, or chef—and you will be successful; you will enjoy every day as if you were not working.

7

Red Lobster: The Beginning

RECIPE FOR LIFE

I believe God guided me in all directions of my life, putting the right opportunities and the right people before me at the right time.

After six remodeling jobs, Gary's Duck Inn had grown to cover almost a quarter acre of dining rooms, with seating for four hundred. But as the roads into Orlando changed, so did the number of customers. Newly built interstates were diverting tourist traffic. South Orange Blossom Trail was being ignored. Gary's Duck Inn would hang on until October of 1994 but would ultimately close after forty-nine years of business.

But the tradition and history remain. With the experience and the understanding gained at Gary's Duck Inn, Bill Darden, Wally Buckley, and I were able to create a new casual dining concept. And that concept would ultimately grow into more than seven hundred locations worldwide.

The fact is, back in the heyday of Gary's Duck Inn, there were really only a few different types of restaurants. In the suburbs, there were primarily mom-and-pop restaurants and fast-food joints, while bigger cities had luncheonettes and supper clubs. There were fancy, white-tablecloth fine-dining restaurants on one end, and quick-service, greasy-spoon diners on the other. Gary's gave me the idea to start thinking in terms of something new: a chain of restaurants that would enable diners to sit down and eat a meal quickly and inexpensively—a casual family dining experience.

The thing is, I knew that Gary's was making more bottom-line money than the Thunderbird. The Thunderbird had a head chef, a baker, a butcher, white linen tablecloths, and ongoing maintenance. Seems we were always replacing carpet or redoing a room. Gary's was simpler. Certainly, I thought, we could take advantage of that simplicity for our new restaurant idea.

Wally Buckley knew of a popular local oyster bar, so we went and sat there and watched and studied their operation. Then we integrated what we learned there with the casual dining concept of Gary's Duck Inn and developed a game plan for our casual seafood restaurant. Wally helped me to refine the ideas and systems necessary to sell the concept to Bill Darden.

Bill was a smart guy and conservative when it came to money. He knew finance, and he was good at talking to bankers and negotiating leases. He and I complemented each other well in that regard. I knew food, and I had the ideas. Bill knew the money side of the equation. When he got on board with our idea, I knew we were on to something special.

At the start, the dream was to have a chain of casual seafood restaurants in the Southeast. We had evidence that seafood restaurants worked on the coast, but would seafood appeal to landlocked America? We selected Lakeland, Florida, as the test market. It was a sleepy little town in the center of the state, and we felt if it would go there, it would go anywhere.

We planned an economical seafood menu, eliminated all the costly extras such as place mats, bread and butter, and dessert. I hired Bob Wolf of the E. H. Thompson Restaurant Equipment House to develop a floor plan that would ensure fast service. We didn't want it to be a fish camp. We

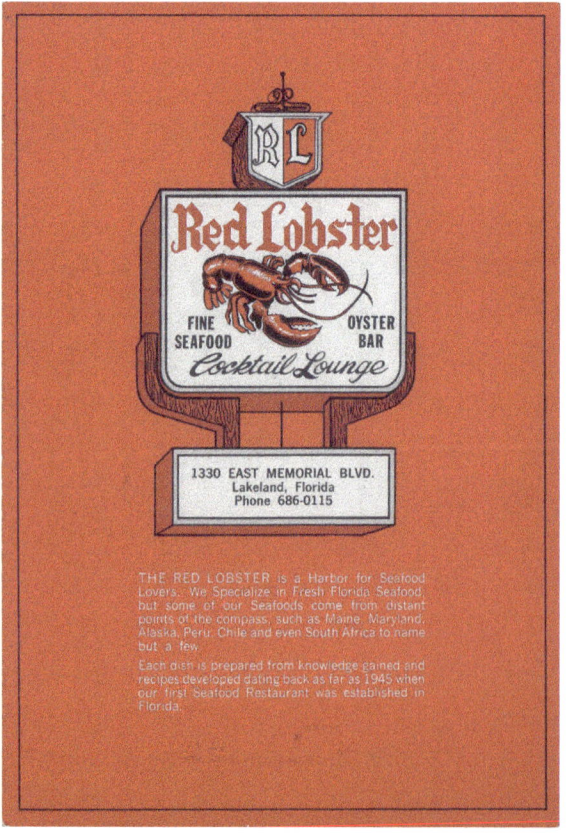

First Red Lobster menu cover, 1968 (Courtesy of Red Lobster)

wanted to be above that but not pricey. In fact, the original motto was "Informal, family priced."

We wanted to deliver great hospitality, high-quality service, steaming-hot food, affordable prices, and freshness. For that first location in Lakeland, we borrowed several of Gary's recipes, such as cocktail sauce, hush puppies, tartar sauce, coleslaw, and salad dressing. We also didn't accept credit cards, to keep the costs down. When we would eventually open in January of 1968, we could brag that a family of four could eat for twelve bucks.

But before opening, we had one unresolved issue: the name. We had started construction on the building before we even had one. I had a yellow legal pad in my office in Jacksonville at the Thunderbird full of pages of restaurant names that all my friends and the wait staff had suggested. One morning the local printer who was preparing the Thunderbird menus came in and saw me leafing through the pad and asked what I was doing. I said I was trying to name an informal family-priced seafood restaurant in Lakeland. He suggested Red Lobster. "When lobsters are cooked, they turn red," he said.

"Well, lobster is too upscale for what we're doing," I replied.

"No, it's not really," he maintained. "You ought to consider it."

The more I repeated the name to myself, the more it jumped out. I ran it by Bill and a few of the partners. Bill wasn't sold on it right away, but soon enough everybody agreed that the name seemed to have a good ring to it; it was easy to pronounce, recognize, and remember. We had a vote, and "Red Lobster" it was.

Outside the first Red Lobster, Lakeland, Florida, opened on January 18, 1968

RECIPE FOR LIFE

Teddy Roosevelt stated that the only one who never makes a mistake is the one who never does anything.

8

Hitting It Big

RECIPE FOR LIFE

Listen to your employees; you can always learn from them.

Lakeland was in Polk County, a county that had a good-sized population—approximately 250,000 people. It was an established community with several nice restaurants and family restaurants too, but there was a lack of renowned seafood restaurants. We knew Lakeland could be a good test for us.

The location was a corner on Lake Parker and Lake View, a promising piece of land in the suburbs. Wally had found it driving around on his day off. We leased it from two local law partners, Lawton Chiles and Bill Ellsworth. Chiles would one day go on to become governor of Florida. The lease was a flat rate plus a percentage of overage on sales. This ended up being a really good deal for our landlords. We did well, so they did well too. Then, with profits from Gary's Duck Inn, we put $100,000 into the building. We had an eye-catching sign designed for $5,000 that we paid for out of the first month's profits.

Interior of first Red Lobster (Courtesy of Red Lobster)

The interior of that first restaurant sported gray walls with a sparsely furnished, informal nautical flair of fish scenes from Florida and New England, Armstrong brick tile, and Formica tables.

We billed it as a "harbor for seafood lovers." The menu included a variety of seafood specialties. Seafood was plentiful and low cost at the time, but you couldn't really get it except on the coast. We secured the best seafood possible from the best places in the world. We bought the best shrimp at seventy-five cents a pound. The Florida Coast shrimp were always my favorite, so long as they were available. When those weren't around, we switched to the Bay of Campeche in the Yucatan, which had incredibly sweet white shrimp. I loved the flounder from Canada and Nova Scotia, which we used to get at thirty-one to thirty-two cents per pound, beautiful fillets without pin bones. Scallops were from the same area as the flounder. Grouper came from Progresso, Mexico.

Bill wanted to serve ice cream because of his Howard Johnson experience, but we ultimately decided against it. We'd watched customers at Gary's Duck Inn order one dessert per table and drink refills of coffee, often occupying their tables for an additional fifteen minutes or more. Our concept was to turn the tables in thirty to forty minutes. I told Bill that we would put some space in the kitchen for an ice cream cabinet, and if we decided later that we needed to serve dessert, we would. After we started operations, Bill came around to agreeing with our strategy of no desserts when he saw how quickly we were turning tables.

Other plans included keeping the ticket time in the kitchen to ten minutes. Seventy-five percent of the menu featured fried items that cooked very quickly. The check was placed on the table at the time the food was delivered and the bill settled only in cash. To maintain the family restaurant atmosphere, we didn't use trays, only arm service. We didn't use place mats or tablecloths, either. Finally, we kept the menu simple and easy to read for quicker service.

Joe Lee, who had been managing the Green Frog, came to work at that first Red Lobster on day one, and he never left the Red Lobster business. Joe had completed a stint with the Air Force Academy and was headed to Valdosta State College. He was on summer break during that first year of our Red Lobster, and I had a long talk with him, letting him know we were on to something that seemed very promising. So, rather than heading back to Georgia, Joe joined the team, which by then already included me, Wally Buckley, Al Woods, Bill Darden, Denham Darden, and later Gus Gornto.

Joe started as an assistant manager and moved up quickly to the manager's post. Joe became a key member of that early crew. I don't guess he had any regrets about not going back to Valdosta State. Later, he'd go on to become CEO and chairman, leading the company through much of its growth. Eventually, he'd even be elected to the board of directors of General Mills. Joe learned the restaurant business well. He knew how to deal with people, "implementing a Southeast Georgia culture of honesty and treating employees, customers, and suppliers well."[7]

And that in a nutshell was the key: good people. We were blessed to have the right people in the right jobs at the right time. It was truly a team effort. And it paid off. The public's response to the Red Lobster idea was overwhelming. As Al Woods would put it years later in an interview, "We were absolutely crushed with people coming to try the new restaurant and the line outside started at 4:00 p.m. when the restaurant did not open for another hour. They would come four or five times the first week saying that they would have to eat there one more time because of the price value before they go broke."[8]

No one anticipated immediate expansion, but we knew we had hit it big.

Uniforms from the first Red Lobster in Lakeland, Florida, worn by JoAnn Livesay, Harriett Taber, and Agnes Taylor

---

[7] "General Mills, Inc.: New Board Member," Deanne Brandon, *Orlando Sentinel*, September 26, 1985.

[8] "Alfred T. Woods, 81, Was a Founder of Red Lobster," Sharon McBreen, *Orlando Sentinel*, December 12, 1992.

Bill Darden, me, and Joe Lee

RECIPE FOR LIFE

Believe you can, and you can.

9

Expansion

RECIPE FOR LIFE

I have a strong passion that compelled and ruled me by an intense emotion that produced an understanding of how to surpass all expectations; how to do great food was the best motivation of all. It was a great treat to walk through the dining room and see all the happy people enjoying wonderful food.

Success arrived so fast that the first expansion came in two weeks; all the kitchen equipment had to be replaced with higher-speed, higher-capacity equipment. We already had loans from the bank, but we had to borrow more to expand the restaurant.

The kitchen had five fryers, and breading shrimp and cooking all day were so tough that people would burn out and disappear—sometimes right in the middle of their shifts. During a trip to Greenville, South Carolina, I found a place that had making hush puppies down to a science. All the hush puppies were uniform. I had never seen it like that, and so I snuck into the kitchen and saw the thing over the deep fat fryer. As the hush puppies came out, they fell into the hot grease. We were using spoons, and it was taking two guys to keep up with the hush puppies at our Red Lobster. The hush puppy machine was the solution I'd been looking for.

The real key was, of course, the seafood menu. The timing was perfect. McDonald's was serving the Little Gordon Fish Sandwich, and Frisch's Big Boy had a couple of operations. And that was it for affordable, family seafood. Nobody knew what shrimp was, and when we opened the Red Lobster, we had no idea of making it a national chain until after we saw the incredible response.

To handle the incredible volume and maintain consistent flavors, I went to Griffith Laboratories to work with Chef Otto, and we started the development of all the original Red Lobster seasonings, from seafood seasoning for broiled fish and seafood to a one-step shrimp-breading process and hush puppy mix where you just added water to it. I also worked with Bell Seafood Jacksonville for crab stuffing and with Eastern Foods Atlanta for the coleslaw, salad dressings, cocktail sauce, and tartar sauce.

Those early days were tremendously busy, and I found myself working twelve- to fourteen-hour days. In that first year, I spent my birthday in the kitchen of the restaurant. It was just a month after we'd opened. Jean and the kids came down from Jacksonville to spend the day with me, but I couldn't leave. In fact, our dishwasher didn't show up that day, so I told Jean to take Ron to the Ramada where I'd been staying, put him into some dungarees, and bring him back to the restaurant to wash dishes! He and I worked until two in the morning. For the first two months of operation, I never took a day off.

The hard work paid off. By 1970, we had three Red Lobsters in operation, all in Central Florida, and two more under construction. Despite our name, it was the fried fish and hush puppies favored by southerners that brought in an average of $1 million each in annual sales. From the start! I remember expecting about $300,000 for that first restaurant in the first year, and hitting $1 million was amazing. A $1 million restaurant was unheard of in those days. Over the next twenty-four months, the success in Lakeland would be repeated in Daytona Beach, Orlando, Tampa, and Saint Petersburg.

One way to keep our food affordable and thus to continue to separate us from the tablecloth restaurants was to promote whatever seafood was the best buy at the time. But we wanted quality too. This took some work and some travel on my part. In Mexico, when I went down there, I noticed the fishermen would go out in a rowboat, stay out a couple of days catching fish, and throw them into the boat without ice. They brought the fish back to a little warehouse where the women would come in and process them. The fish were then placed in a freezer that took a couple of days to thoroughly freeze the fish. Since this took so long, the fish were considered old because of the mishandling. I recommended they get ice machines so they could take ice out with them on the boat. I also suggested they purchase tunnel freezers so they could quick-freeze with nitrogen, also known as blast freezing. This process ensured that we received fresh frozen grouper out of Mexico.

All the seafood was brought in by truck to the regional warehouse. Quality control would check the entire load from front, middle, and back. Flounder was checked for pin bones. One box from each section of the truck went through the test kitchen and was inspected and cooked. A young man by the name of Walter King ran the test kitchen.

I'd hired him previously at the Thunderbird. He was African American, and we were proud of the fact that in a time when discrimination was still occurring, we provided opportunities for anybody.

After testing, the product was then placed in the freezer in the warehouse and distributed to each restaurant as needed. As we opened more restaurants, we opened regional distribution centers. The first four were Orlando, Atlanta, Dallas, and Saint Louis.

Training was important too. Ed Chatham headed up the first Red Lobster training class for what we called the "Red Lobster Way." Of course many of the original employees had grown up at Gary's Duck Inn. Like Bonnie Lynch. She and I wrote the first Red Lobster training manual for opening the front of the house. Joe Lee and I wrote the manual for the back of the house, as well as the manager's training program. Job descriptions were written for each position. Later, when we really started to expand throughout the Southeast, Bonnie would travel to each new restaurant to train them on our "Red Lobster Way."

We rewarded people who worked hard. There were many examples of people moving quickly up the ladder, like Richard Tourigny, who started out as a busboy while in high school and shortly made his way to area supervisor.

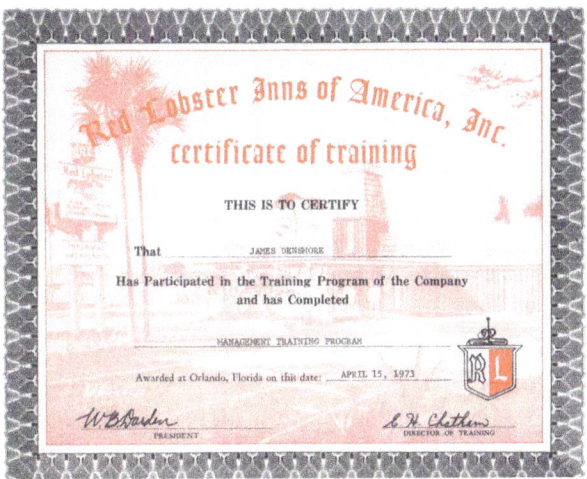

Richard Tourigny started as a busboy in Lakeland, Florida, his senior year of high school. He became an area supervisor.

Original Red Lobster Menu

May we suggest your Favorite Cocktail!!

MARTINI
MANHATTAN
WHISKEY SOUR
OLD FASHION
DAQUIRI
COLLINS

65¢

After Dinner

Creme De Menthe	.55
Creme De Cocoa	.55
Cointreau	.65
Benedictine	.65
Cherry Brandy	.65
Blackberry Brandy	.65
Apricot Brandy	.65
B & B	.85
Cherry Heering	.85
Anisette	.70
Kahlua	.80
Drambuie	.85

Beer

MILLER'S ON DRAUGHT
16 oz. Schooner	.35
Pitcher of Beer	.75

HEINEKEN ON DRAUGHT
Stein of Beer	.55
Pitcher of Beer	1.40

WINE LIST ON TABLES

Beverages

Coffee	.15
Milk	.20
Iced or Hot Tea	.15
Soft Drinks	.15

* * * * *

RAPID SERVICE, NO WAITING ON TAKE HOME ORDERS

TOSSED SALAD as Salad Substitute on Entrees 20c

OYSTERS

OYSTERS ON THE HALF SHELL ½ Dozen .65	One Dozen 1.25
OYSTER COCKTAIL — Raw oysters with our tangy cocktail sauce	.75
OYSTER STEW — Chuck full of plump oysters in half and half milk	.85
FRIED OYSTERS — ½ dozen fried selects	.80
With Hush Puppies, choice of Potato and Cole Slaw	1.25
One dozen selects	1.45
With Hush Puppies, choice of Potato and Cole Slaw	1.85
OYSTER SANDWICH — Golden fried selects on a bun	.50

SHRIMP

SHRIMP COCKTAIL — Fresh chilled shrimp with tangy cocktail sauce	.75
SHRIMP BOILED IN BEER — Fresh Florida shrimp in the shell, cooked in beer, served hot or cold with hush puppies and sauce	1.35
SAUTEED SHRIMP — Fresh Florida shrimp sauteed in garlic butter with hush puppies, choice of Potato and Cole Slaw	1.65
HALF DOZEN GOLDEN FRIED SHRIMP — Side Dish	.60
SHRIMP SALAD COLD PLATE	1.50
SHRIMP SANDWICH — Golden fried shrimp on a bun	.50
FRIED SHRIMP — One dozen golden fried shrimp	1.10
With Hush Puppies, choice of Potato and Cole Slaw	1.35

CRAB

FLORIDA CRAB MEAT COCKTAIL — With tangy cocktail sauce	.75
FLORIDA CRAB COCKTAIL FINGERS — With tangy cocktail sauce	.85
ALASKAN KING CRAB MEAT COCKTAIL — With tangy cocktail sauce	.95
LUMP CRAB MEAT SALAD	1.50
SAUTEED KING CRAB MEAT — Succulent king crab sauteed in butter with Hush Puppies, Choice of Potato and Cole Slaw	1.95
FRIED FLORIDA CRAB CLAW FINGERS — With Hush Puppies, choice of Potato and Cole Slaw	1.35
FRIED CRAB CAKES (4) — With Hush Puppies, choice of Potato and Cole Slaw	1.25
BROILED KING CRAB LEGS, DRAWN BUTTER — With Hush Puppies, choice of Potato and Cole Slaw	2.50

CLAMS

CLAMS ON THE HALF SHELL ½ Dozen .65	One Dozen 1.25
CHOWDER — Steaming bowl of New England cream style chowder. Chuck full of tender clams Cup .35	Bowl .60
FRIED CLAM DINNER — Tender and sweet, with choice of Potato and Cole Slaw	1.50
FRIED CLAM SANDWICH	.50

Due to our Price Structure

(Courtesy of Red Lobster)

(Courtesy of Red Lobster)

RECIPE FOR LIFE

What you sow, you will reap; sow seeds to help others.

10

An Amazing Time

RECIPE FOR LIFE

*Surround yourself with good people. Set goals.
Be a friend with your employees; don't act like you are above them.*

By 1970, we owned and operated five restaurants in Florida: Lakeland, Daytona Beach, Tampa, Saint Petersburg, and Winter Park. There was a sixth about to open in Gainesville, another was planned for Clearwater, and more were under contract. There were also franchises in Georgia and South Carolina. By then, we knew our concept could go nationwide. We kept working in the "Red Lobster Way" to create the culture that would soon convince food giant General Mills that the new restaurant chain could do well from coast to coast. Inside the restaurants, no operations or customer service detail escaped our strict standards. Our team was tightly structured and well disciplined. As it happened, Cape Canaveral was in a downturn, and many engineers and scientists had been recently laid off. This provided us an intelligent and disciplined recruiting pool from which to hire. We were able to develop strong leadership throughout the organization. In fact, many former and current General Mills/Darden restaurant executives got their start by learning the Red Lobster operating fundamentals.

The rapid success of our chain caught the attention of the officials at General Mills at a time when they were looking for an investment in food-related businesses. Actually, it started with a Henny Penny salesman who tipped off Merv Phillips of Griffith

Laboratories about our success. Merv wanted to buy in but couldn't provide the capital we needed to expand as aggressively as we wanted to. We declined, and Merv then mentioned us to General Mills, who sent representatives down to check us out and then ultimately got the whole board involved.

On Thursday, January 8, 1970, through an exchange of stock, General Mills acquired a majority interest in Red Lobster Inns of America. It was a performance contract. We sold under the agreement that we stay with the company for a period of three years to carry out plans for expansion for General Mills. Bill Darden was to continue as president and CEO of Red Lobster, and I was to remain as the executive vice president in charge of operations.

The sale of Red Lobster probably was the height of my success. But, you know, from 1970 to 1973, we saw incredible growth, and I'm just as proud of that. The truth is, the infusion of cash from General Mills allowed us to speed up our expansion across the country.

The acquisition also brought our team into contact with some talented businesspeople. James McFarland was chairman of the board and CEO of General Mills Inc. He'd spent his entire career with General Mills, starting at the company's mill in Wichita, Kansas, in a Depression-era job selling bags of flour and boxes of Wheaties. This would lead ultimately to executive positions and eventually CEO. McFarland helped the Golden Valley food industry giant triple its business to $2.6 billion in the 1970s by diversifying into other markets, like restaurants, toys, and fashion. Red Lobster was not General Mills' first foray into the restaurant business. Others included Betty Crocker Pie Shops, Tree House Restaurants, York's Budget Steakhouses, York's Choices, Hannahans, Fennimore, Union Jack Fish & Chips, and Uncle Don's Barbecue chain. McFarland saw the acquisition of Red Lobster as part of a plan to expand the "away from home eating field."[9]

The years 1970 to 1973 were a blur of activity. Red Lobster was on the map and in a big way. But no such success would have been possible without an incredible team. One key member was contractor Mack Miller. Mack's SE Construction Development Co. received a call in January 1970 from Bud Simms, an independent architect who was in charge of constructing the Red Lobster buildings. Bud invited Mack to bid on a newly planned Tallahassee location. Mack had built a shopping center that Bud had designed and had finished the project thirty-four days ahead of schedule. At that point, not one of the five existing Red Lobster restaurants had been built in less than four months, and most of the units were one to two months late. One site under construction in Atlanta was already thirty days behind the four-month time schedule that General Mills had specified, and there were plans for four more units sitting on Bud's desk. All five of the previous contractors had been barred from the bidding process in Tallahassee.

---

[9] "James McFarland, 90, Executive Who Diversified General Mills," Wolfgang Saxon, *NY Times*, May 15, 2012.

AN AMAZING TIME

Unfortunately, when Mack submitted his bid, he lost out by $400. Wally Buckley was there, and he followed Mack outside after the bidding and said that he was sorry that the figures were off but that the East Semoran location was coming up next. Mack bid again but lost that bid to a large company out of Sanford by a few hundred dollars. Mack assured Bud Simms that he would continue to bid and that he could prove he could construct their buildings in four months or less. His next chance came in Clearwater. He lost that one, too, this time by $324. Nevertheless, there were circumstances with that bid that allowed me to award Mack the project. And Mack quickly demonstrated his efficiency. At the forty-five-day midpoint of the project, the building was six days ahead of schedule.

Mack soon saw a golden opportunity. He approached us with the idea of setting up a construction division owned and controlled within the Red Lobster organization. Mack knew that General Mills hoped to open two sites a month, and much time was being wasted on design, the bidding process, and the process of getting permits. Mack calculated that if each unit was delayed up to ten weeks—as they had been up to that point—based on an income of $20,000 per week (the store average at that time), each store was losing approximately $200,000 in sales. Consequently, if Red Lobster planned for thirty new stores per year, that would equal $6 million in operating losses per year. Moreover, if the ninety-day schedule Mack had in mind was maintained and one month was saved per location, that would *add* an additional $20,000 per month in revenue.

Mack gained assurances that as the sole construction expert on the team, he would have adequate authority to implement his plan. With the prospect of national exposure as an additional incentive, Mack signed on with Red Lobster in June 1970. Bill Darden confided in Mack that had he told General Mills about the hiring, they would have vetoed the idea. They had tried twice before to have a construction department within the company, and both times it had failed. But we were all impressed with Mack's ninety-day progress chart and his ability to explain the process of each phase. Our confidence was not misplaced. Mack organized a completely independent division that could produce a Red Lobster ninety days after the purchase of a site in any city in the country.

In July of 1970, just as our rapid growth began to explode, tragedy struck the team. Bud Simms was killed in a freak accident. When a huge sinkhole opened up in Winter Park, Bud and a friend, who were both deep-sea divers, tried to rescue two little boys who fell in. The hole had such incredible suction pressure that when Bud's friend emerged from the dive, he had to be treated for decompression sickness with emergency equipment rushed from Cape Canaveral. Bud never resurfaced.

Bud's brave efforts to save the young boys left a hole in the Red Lobster organization, but Mack quickly set about the task of finding architects, and the sprint lost no speed. It was an amazing time. In total, we opened seventy stores in the years between 1970 and 1973, with thirty more pieces of property already purchased and awaiting construction.

RED LOBSTER...THE BEGINNING

Food Giant Buys Red Lobster Inns

Operators of the Red Lobster Inns in St. Petersburg and Tampa learned yesterday they now work for General Mills Inc..

"And we don't even serve Wheaties," said one of the employes.

The $885-million food giant announced in Minneapolis it had acquired controlling interest in Red Lobster Inns of America Inc., Orlando-based seafood chain that owns and operates five restaurants in Florida.

BESIDES St. Petersburg and Tampa, Red Lobster has inns in Lakeland, North Daytona and Winter Park. Another is to open soon in Gainesville, and still another was planned for Clearwater. Although present outlets are company-owned, franchising had been planned.

James P. McFarland, General Mills chairman, said the acquisition is a part of the company's program to expand in the away-from-home eating field. He said General Mills will construct and operate six additional restaurants in the Southeast in the next six months.

Organized in 1968, Red Lobster Inns opened its St. Petersburg restaurant at 773 66th St. N only Oct. 9. Cost was put at $330,000. It seats 250 and offers a varied seafood-steak-chicken menu as well as take-out service.

C. D. SPECK, the local restaurant's general manager, said he had heard other companies had made offers for the chain, but the General Mills acquisition — accomplished through an exchange of stock — was a surprise. Another employe said the inn doesn't serve breakfasts, "so we don't serve Wheaties, Cheerios or any of the other foods General Mills is famous for."

Joe Lee, me, Bill Darden, Al Woods, and Mr. Lawton. Lawton was the first manager of the first Red Lobster in Lakeland.

AN AMAZING TIME

Bill Darden and me selling Red Lobster to General Mills[10]

John Laurens, Red Lobster comptroller, awarding Mack Miller on December 22, 1973, for the fastest build-out of a store: fifty-eight days

---

[10] *Orlando Sentinel*, 13 Feb, 1972, p. 8-D

RED LOBSTER...THE BEGINNING

"The Nation's Finest
Seafood Restaurants
Informal & Family Priced"

September 15, 1972

Mr. William Miller
Director of Construction
Central Office

Dear Mr. Miller:

We hope that you will take pride in reviewing the enclosed Annual Report. The progress and growth which Red Lobster Inns of America, Inc. has experienced during the past fiscal year are significant.

More importantly, Mr. Woodsby, Mr. Lee, and the management staff here in Orlando wish to express our sincere appreciation and pride in the personal efforts and contributions on your part which have made Red Lobster Inns one of America's finest and largest family priced restaurant organizations.

As you will note in the Report, Away-from-Home Foods and Red Lobster are rapidly becoming a major factor within General Mills. This is particularly rewarding to me because it means that we will be able to continue to offer more and greater opportunities to those who contribute to our growth and progress.

We face many opportunities and challenges. I am confident that, together, we will continue to be successful in meeting them now and in the years ahead.

Sincerely,

W. B. Darden
President

WBD/mhh

Enclosure

REC'D SEP 1 8 1972

Red Lobster Inns of America, Inc. ■ 6880 Lake Ellenor Drive ■ Orlando, Florida 32809
305/851-0370   (Executive Offices)   P. O. Box 13330

Letter of appreciation from Bill to Mack

RECIPE FOR LIFE

Always hire the best people you can. Maintain high standards, have good character, and make sure they are trained, trained, and trained. Treat your employees right once they are hired.

11

The Rise of Red Lobster and My Retirement

RECIPE FOR LIFE

Running this business is not about me. It is about all the great people that have helped me to grow this business and make it successful.

As we reached more parts of the country, Red Lobster continually introduced guests to fresh dishes that quickly became favorites, with many guests getting their first taste of calamari, snow crab, and key lime pie. (By then, desserts had been added to the menu.) As Joe Lee put it one time, our biggest competition back then was the kitchen stove and people cooking at home. We invented popcorn shrimp, which, as the *New York Times* once reported, drove fried shrimp into its own fad: "It's bite-sized, lightly breaded and golden fried."[11] We introduced hush puppies to Chicago and the Midwest, and they were very well accepted. We had crispy fried calamari, flounder, swordfish, sole, and halibut.

Bill and I also established an in-house purchasing department that could source everything, from restaurant equipment to primary kitchen supplies from EH Thompson to various species of seafood from a worldwide network. Our employees bought seafood directly off the boat only in Saint Petersburg, where processing was supervised. Otherwise,

---

[11] McGill, Douglas C., "Why They Smile at Red Lobster," *New York Times*, April 23, 1989.

we bought from packers who met rigid quality and cleanliness standards with frequent spot checks. I remember that Joe Lee had a slide rule that he carried everywhere in the early 1970s to calculate prices and portion weights, and he also carried a thermometer to ensure that entrees had been cooked to the proper temperature before being served.

Of course I had to have a way to get all this great seafood to the rapidly growing population of raving seafood fans across the country, so I devised a regional distribution system in which seafood was shipped into Orlando, Atlanta, Dallas, and Denver.

Our dramatic growth brought other innovations too. We pioneered the development of what is now commonly referred to as point-of-sale cash register equipment. When minicomputers came out, we thought about how great it would be if there were a computer in each restaurant that could capture information to help us better understand which seafood was selling and which weren't.

The pressure of rapid growth in the 1970s was relentless. Red Lobster grew quickly in each year of operation. At the end of 1971, there were twenty-four restaurants, with sales revenue totaling $9.1 million. At the end of 1972, there were forty-seven, with sales of $27.1 million, and by the end of 1975, there would be ninety-seven restaurants, with 9,500 employees. During one twelve-month period, Red Lobster opened thirty full-service restaurants in one year and was the fastest-growing restaurant company at that time. By 1973, we had opened seventy-five restaurants, and I had approved fifteen more locations.

But life is not a sprint; it's a marathon. I'd been sprinting at full speed for years, and at age forty-two, I found myself spending far too little time with my wife and kids. I remember once taking the family on a holiday weekend to Daytona Beach and spending most of the time in the hotel bed, exhausted. Fortunately for the family, through all the hard work and long days, Jean was a rock. She was strong and family oriented, and even though I missed out on a lot of family activities in those years, we still managed to successfully raise three kids on strong family values. My work ethic rubbed off on all of them. And no matter how busy I was, the kids knew they were loved. Anytime I was around on Sunday mornings, we'd go to church as a family. It helped too that Jean's mother lived with us. She provided a little extra glue to keep the family strong.

Now it was time for a change of pace. After much soul searching, I decided to leave Red Lobster at the end of my three-year commitment. Building on our early blueprint, Red Lobster continued to grow. In 1975, Bill Darden was promoted to the position of vice president of operations for the restaurant unit, and Joe Lee, the company's first restaurant manager, was made president of Red Lobster. I knew I'd left the organization in great hands.

TO: DISTRIBUTION
DATE: MAY 25, 1973
SUBJECT: CHARLES E. WOODSBY

IT IS WITH DEEP REGRET THAT WE ARE ANNOUNCING THE RETIREMENT OF CHARLES E. WOODSBY. HIS RETIREMENT WILL BE EFFECTIVE AS OF THE END OF THIS CURRENT FISCAL YEAR ON MAY 28TH.

AS YOU ARE AWARE, CHARLIE IS ONE OF THE ORIGINAL FOUNDERS OF RED LOBSTER. CHARLIE ACTIVELY PARTICIPATED IN THE CREATION AND OPENING OF THE FIRST RED LOBSTER IN LAKELAND --- THE RESTAURANT THAT WAS THE BEGINNING OF WHAT IS TODAY THE WORLD'S LARGEST SEAFOOD RESTAURANT CHAIN.

I'M SURE YOU ALL JOIN ME IN WISHING CHARLIE WELL IN THE FUTURE AND LOOK BACK FONDLY AT OUR EXPERIENCES OVER THE YEARS.

Bill

W. B. DARDEN

Letter from Bill Darden

GENERAL MILLS, INC. • EXECUTIVE OFFICES • 9200 Wayzata Boulevard • Minneapolis, Minnesota

J. P. McFARLAND
Chairman of the Board
Chief Executive Officer

PERSONAL

June 11, 1973

Mr. Charles Woodsby
Red Lobster Inns of America, Inc.
6880 Lake Ellenor Drive
Orlando, Florida 32809

Dear Charlie:

I appreciated so very much your wonderful letter of June 4, and I can assure you that we are exceedingly sorry to have you leave Red Lobster and we'll miss you greatly.

Our association with Bill, you, and all the other wonderful people of Red Lobster has been one of the great highlights of my business life, and we look forward to outstanding experiences ahead as we mutually grow and develop.

You should take great pride and satisfaction in seeing the development which has taken place to date. You have been a very major part, of course, in setting the base for our future growth and development in those areas.

I know you are going to have great success and happiness in your new activities and I shall look forward to every opportunity to see you along the way.

Warm wishes for a great future.

Sincerely,

Jim

JPM:pml

Letter from Jim McFarland

RECIPE FOR LIFE

You become the way in which you think. If you think negatively, you'll become negative. If you think positively, you'll become positive.

12

The Red Lobster Legacy

RECIPE FOR LIFE

My legacy in the restaurant industry is to provide great-quality food at prices the average family can afford...so they can eat out.

After my retirement, Red Lobster just kept growing. It was immensely gratifying to watch, and I continued to feel proud of what I'd helped start. I was proud too of all of the people who had contributed to Red Lobster's success. Success on that scale takes a team of dedicated, creative, devoted people. I knew I was blessed to be affiliated with such a wonderful group of professionals and friends.

In 1976 Red Lobster ended the fiscal year with 174 units in twenty-six states and total sales of $174.1 million. About that time, the company felt the need to upgrade, so the floors were carpeted, the interiors were lightened up, and a few fresh dishes were added to the predominantly frozen menu. Prices were raised to pay for these upgrades, and the strategy worked. By the end of 1980, with 260 units and almost $400 million in annual sales, Red Lobster had reached ninth place among fast-food companies and accounted for more than half of total sales by seafood fast-food companies. (Although a sit-down chain, frequently with lounges, it was considered "fast food" by some analysts.)

Meanwhile, expansion continued. Because of the incredible amount of detail in the construction of the new restaurants, Sigma Con was formed as part of General Mills to design and build the new facilities. The president of Sigma Con was Peter Markham, who directed construction work at Walt Disney World in Orlando. He joined Red Lobster in 1974 as director of construction.

In January of 1979, William Hattaway became president when Joe Lee moved up to the parent company. By the end of that year, Red Lobster was the world's largest buyer of commercial shrimp, at around nine million pounds a year. All told, the director of purchasing, Jonathan Sleik, bought thirty-five million pounds of seafood in 1979. By 1981, with three hundred stores, annual sales averaged close to $1 million per store. By 1982, Red Lobster was rated as the nation's largest "dinner house" restaurant chain, this being the term for a restaurant offering table service and a full lunch and dinner menu. With an average annual return on invested assets of 22.3 percent before taxes, it was one of the most profitable chains in its field.

In 1985, a big emphasis was placed on ten varieties of fresh fish by experimenting with retail fish markets through an iced fresh-fish counter to capitalize on diners' increasing quality demands for takeout food. As part of the new takeout business, Red Lobster pushed the Clambake to Go, a strong sell in most retail fish markets. This was a tin filled with lobster, shrimp, clams, and mussels that could be heated on the stove. The price started at around $11.95.[12]

In March of 1986, Hattaway took over as chairman and CEO of Red Lobster Inns of America Inc. and enthusiastically talked about the company's plans to build new restaurants. He also laid out his vision for a restructuring that was designed to speed up the growth of General Mills Restaurant Group, a division of General Mills Inc. The reorganization pulled the international division under Hattaway's authority. The hopes were to add thirty-four units in Canada to the five existing ones by the end of the year. There were five in Japan, which were part of a joint venture, with intentions for seven more by the end of 1986. One of Hattaway's goals was to have five hundred Red Lobsters in the United States by 1990.[13] But in 1989, he decided to leave the organization, feeling it wasn't being aggressive enough in its growth. From there, Hattaway would go on to become president and CEO of Shells Seafood Restaurants.

In 1993, Jeff O'Hara became president of Red Lobster USA. He had started his career in 1970 as an assistant manager for a Betty Crocker Tree House Restaurant and Bakeshop. Following a two-year stint in the navy, he returned to General Mills as an assistant manager at Red Lobster. Upon earning a college degree in marketing, O'Hara was assigned to the headquarters of Red Lobster. Jim Doherty, who was the head of the marketing department and a fellow Betty Crocker Tree House refugee, picked O'Hara to be a marketing analyst. O'Hara quickly settled in. In 1976 he took charge of the

---

[12] Vicki Vaughn, "Red Lobster Hooks onto a New Attitude, Seafood Chain Shores Up Organization, Tastes," *Orlando Sentinel*, March 24, 1986.

[13] Ibid.

twenty-five-person marketing staff, and by 1981 grew it more than sixfold by identifying markets ripe for expansion. He helped produce the chain's most famous jingle, "Red Lobster: for the seafood lover in you." Joe Lee remarked that "the 2-½ year campaign beat all expectations" and proved that O'Hara was an innovator in restaurant marketing.[14]

Jeff O'Hara changed the standing strategy of building in cities with populations of a hundred thousand or more and took on new markets by entering smaller communities, as well as continuing to build in the big-city markets. He also attempted to battle the high cost of real estate with the idea of leasing space in a large hotel or converting a hotel restaurant to save money. He made some other changes, including carpeting over the old floors, making other upgrades, and accepting credit cards.[15]

The Red Lobster family lost one of its titans when Bill Darden passed away on March 29, 1994, after an extended illness. And I lost a friend. Joe Lee called me one day to talk about the company, and he asked if I had any objection to using Bill Darden's name for the new corporation. I thought about it for a few minutes and decided it would be a great honor and wished him the best.

In 1995, General Mills spun off its restaurant division as an independent, publicly traded corporation. It was the one-year anniversary of Bill's death. Joe Lee took the helm of the new corporation. Having developed "the family seafood restaurant" with overwhelming acceptance and decades of incredible growth and success, Red Lobster joined Olive Garden and other sister chains to become part of Darden Restaurants, a $3.2 billion enterprise.[16]

But things began turning for the chain, and not for the better. In June 1997, Darden president and COO Jeff O'Hara resigned. Chairman and CEO Joe Lee became interim president of Red Lobster after a difficult year where operating income dropped by more than half. The company closed the books with a $91 million loss. Forty-eight restaurants were closed, including twenty-six outlets in Canada.

In December 1997, Darden hired turnaround expert Dick Rivera as president of Red Lobster. Joe Lee said that "one of the things we did not keep pace with was the overall experience in the restaurant, the friendliness, the energy level, and the appropriate merchandising of alcoholic beverages. Dick, with his previous involvement at T.G.I. Friday's, brought us a lot of experience in that area."[17]

---

[14] Jim DeSimone, "Darden Chief Has Recipes for Change: Jeff O'Hara's Ideas Bolster Red Lobster, Olive Garden," *Orlando Sentinel*, October 23, 1995.

[15] Vicki Vaughn, "Red Lobster Hooks onto a New Attitude, Seafood Chain Shores Up Organization, Tastes," *Orlando Sentinel*, March 24, 1986.

[16] Jill Krueger, "Popcorn Shrimp and POS: Red Lobster's First 30 Years," *Orlando Business Journal*, January 19, 1998.

[17] Ibid.

In June 1999, the company reported a rebound and was back on track after closing thirteen underperforming restaurants. In April 2002, Dick Rivera was promoted to vice chairman, and Edna Morris was promoted to president of Red Lobster. The good days were back, and Red Lobster enjoyed a profitable decade. In September 2012, Clarence Otis announced that Red Lobster would add five hundred new restaurants in the next five years and hire fifty thousand new employees. As of today there are nearly seven hundred Red Lobster locations throughout the United States and Canada. It's a legacy I'm proud of.

RECIPE FOR LIFE

Thought is the most tremendous force in the universe.

13

Every Step of the Way

RECIPE FOR LIFE

It is important to be passionate and have a hands-on management style. There is true inspiration in a well-trained employee that can learn to do the position so well that the pride is strong and never ending. That is what we instilled in our employees. We had employees that had been with us over forty years.

When I left Red Lobster, I thought I'd take it easy and enjoy an early retirement. I purchased a forty-one-foot Hatteras boat and planned for a life of fishing and being out on the water. That idea lasted all of six months, no longer than it took me to realize that I had no one to play with! All my friends were earning a living, and they wanted to spend their weekends catching up on family time. I also enjoyed golf and tennis but had only senior citizens to play golf with and only women to play tennis. I dabbled in real estate but without any enthusiasm.

One day, I was shooting pool with a businessman friend of mine named Andy Williams, and I confessed, "Andy, I am bored out of my mind, and the only thing I know about is the restaurant business." Andy told me about an old Howard Johnson in Lakeland that had been converted into a struggling spaghetti restaurant that could be had for a good price. I'd signed a noncompete agreement with General Mills that prohibited me from opening a seafood restaurant, but it didn't prevent me from opening a different kind of restaurant. Refreshed by a few months off, I began to dream again—this time about a steak house.

There was another factor that drew me back into business: my son, Ron. Ron had recently returned home from a stint in the US Marine Corps. When I encouraged him to start thinking about college, he said, "Dad, I don't want to waste your money, and I don't want to waste my time. I know what I want to do; I want to be in the restaurant business. You can teach me more than I could ever learn in college."

Ron had actually been in the restaurant business his whole life, cutting his teeth as a youngster at the Old South. By the time he had graduated from high school, he had worked every position in the restaurant: hosting and greeting, running the cash register, and manning every station in the kitchen from the grill to the fryer to the pastry oven. He had also worked at Gary's Duck Inn. So I'd taken Ron under my tutelage. The first lesson: learn from others. At my suggestion, Ron worked at several local restaurants, studying their operation—the efficiency of the kitchen layout and how many steps were required of the workers. Ron worked on the opening team of some of the early Red Lobsters. Then I bought a small restaurant in Lakeland for him to run. Now, as I pondered getting back into business at age forty-three, I saw the opportunity to continue to work alongside Ron as my talented son developed his skills as a restaurateur.

Less than a year after I retired from Red Lobster, in 1973, Ron and I formed a 49–51 partnership and bought that old Howard Johnson Andy Williams had mentioned. We took the trademark orange roof off the building and began a complete renovation. When I went across the street to the tool rental company to lease a jackhammer, the manager asked me why I needed it. I said I was planning on opening a new restaurant across the street, and the man coolly wished me good luck, reminding me that several restaurants in the same space had all failed. I told him, "Well, this one will succeed because it will be the talk of the town."

Ron and I gutted and expanded the building, increased the parking, and put in landscaping that would soon win a town-beautification award. There was a line out the door on opening day in January 1974, and soon the reputation of the restaurant location had been transformed. Soon after, the tool man across the street reported to me that a customer had called to inquire about the location of his own store, to which he'd answered, "Across from the old Howard Johnson." The customer had replied, "You mean the new Talk of the Town restaurant?"

We had a winning concept: a simple steak house with a small salad bar, steak or prime rib, baked potato, and bread. Talk of the Town was open for lunch and dinner, with me managing one shift and Ron the other. As time went on, the menu expanded a bit, and the concept grew. Seafood was added to the menu once my five-year agreement with General Mills expired. Over the next five years, Ron and I opened additional restaurants in Winter Haven, Clearwater, Saint Petersburg, and Orlando.

We experimented a little. The Clearwater location featured a disco that was open late, for instance. But soon we sold the disco and focused on the basic steak house idea.

In 1984 we developed the Texas Cattle Company concept at a time when Longhorn was just getting started and Outback didn't yet exist. A group of Atlanta investors offered us the opportunity to open six Texas Cattle Company sites in Atlanta, but neither one of us wanted a life of traveling back and forth. No doubt we could have created another substantial chain and sold to a large corporation, but we decided instead to focus on Central Florida, developing multiple dining concepts within this growing market.

Over the years, I've stepped back further and further while Ron has become the visionary, guiding one of America's leading family restaurant groups. Talk of the Town now features several high-end steak houses with the highest quality and standards. Three locations—in Orlando, Celebration, and Tampa—bear my name: Charley's Steak House.

Ron has also led the family back to its roots in seafood with the establishment of the award-winning FishBones in Orlando in 1994 and Lake Mary in 2005, and MoonFish in Orlando in 2002. Vito's Chop House, with its inimitable New York Italian style, opened in 1998, and Johnnie's Hideaway, the Florida-themed gem, opened in 2008. Texas Cattle Company locations in Lakeland and Saint Petersburg round out the Talk of the Town family of restaurants, which has over a thousand employees and an annual revenue of $64 million.

On a personal level, in the intervening years, I had lost my biggest supporter. Jean, who had stood by me through thick and thin, passed away in 2004. For fifty-four years,

MaryLou and me

she had been my soul mate. But blessed as my life has been, a second soul mate came along. MaryLou and I are now in our eleventh year of marriage.

As for the restaurant business, it's enormously gratifying to see my legacy living on in the passion that Ron brings to Talk of the Town. Ron is now responsible for all aspects of the restaurant operations. He designs, builds, and equips all the restaurants, focusing on everything from the menu and wine selections to tablecloths and dishes and the artwork and style of doorknobs. He is totally immersed in the process when he builds a new venue, even living in a motor home on the job site while he studies the demographics of the surrounding community. This way he becomes a part of the community he will service and learns the market firsthand. In my mind, he's the best; he really is. He has always had a passion for the restaurant business and is a real student of it. I'd put him up against any restaurateur in the country.

And that's not just my opinion. The Woodsby restaurants have won the Achievement of Excellence Award from the American Culinary Federation. Charley's Steak House has also been on America's top-ten steak house list every year since 1995. It has held the number-one spot in the country since 2007. All the Charley's Steak Houses, as well as Vito's Chop House, have received the Distinguished Restaurants of North America (DiRoNA) Award of Excellence. FishBones has made Tom Horan's America's Top Ten Seafood Houses list since the list's inception in 2001 and was awarded the DiRoNA in 2008. FishBones was inducted into the Seafood Hall of Fame in 2006, and MoonFish was named to Tom Horan's list in 2006 and awarded the DiRoNA the same year. Johnnie's Hideaway is also a recipient of the coveted DiRoNA award.

I'm also proud of what we've given back to the community. These days, I spend most of my time managing the Woodsby Foundation, which Jean and I formed and MaryLou and I now direct. The foundation supports underprivileged children and families in Central Florida and elsewhere. I've also chosen to focus on religious organizations that share the message of faith in God on which I've built my life. I feel that all my life God has directed me. God has had a hand in my life the whole way. A lot of people say, "Hey, I did it. I did it. I did it. If it wasn't for me, this wouldn't have happened." But everything I have I owe to God. He's the one who gave me the vision and direction about where to go and when and how. He has been with me every step of the way.

RECIPE FOR LIFE

Embrace your dreams with passion. One person with passion is better than a hundred with only an interest. Believe you can, and you can.

RED LOBSTER...THE BEGINNING

TALK OF THE TOWN
Established 1974

Good old fashioned food... Good old fashioned fun...
Good old fashioned LOW prices...

Dinner at Talk of the Town

STEAKS	Broiled Beef Shish Kabob	4.50
	New Yorker Strip Steak	6.95
	Petite Filet Mignon	5.25
	Talk of the Town Pepper Steak	3.95
	Steak on a Skewer	3.95
	He-Man Top Sirloin	5.25
	Ground Sirloin Steak	3.25
	Roast Prime Rib of Beef	5.95
	Steak and Danish	5.95
	Steak and Crab	5.95
	Ground Sirloin (Children's Portions 12 and under)	1.75
	Jr. Beef Kabob (Children's Portions 12 and under)	2.25
SEAFOOD	Alaskan King Crab	5.75
	Seafood Feast	6.95
	Baked Fresh Snapper	4.25
	Sauteed Shrimp	4.25
	Danish Lobster	5.95

All entrees include salad bar and homestyle bread.

Talk of the Town

Purveyors of steak, seafood, spirits and FUN!

735 E. Main St., Lakeland • 686-1434
SR 544 & U.S. 17 (Formerly the Landmark), Winter Haven • 293-0423

HOURS:
Lunch Mon-Fri 11:30 AM - 2:00 PM
Sun 11:30 AM - 5:00 PM
Dinner Mon - Thur 5:00 PM - 10:00 PM
Fri - Sat 5:00 PM - 11:00 PM
Sun 5:00 PM - 9:30 PM

We honor BankAmericard, Master Charge, and American Express.

Ron Woodsby at the first Orlando opening

RESTAURANTS

TEXAS CATTLE COMPANY
Lakeland
Established 1984

RED LOBSTER...THE BEGINNING

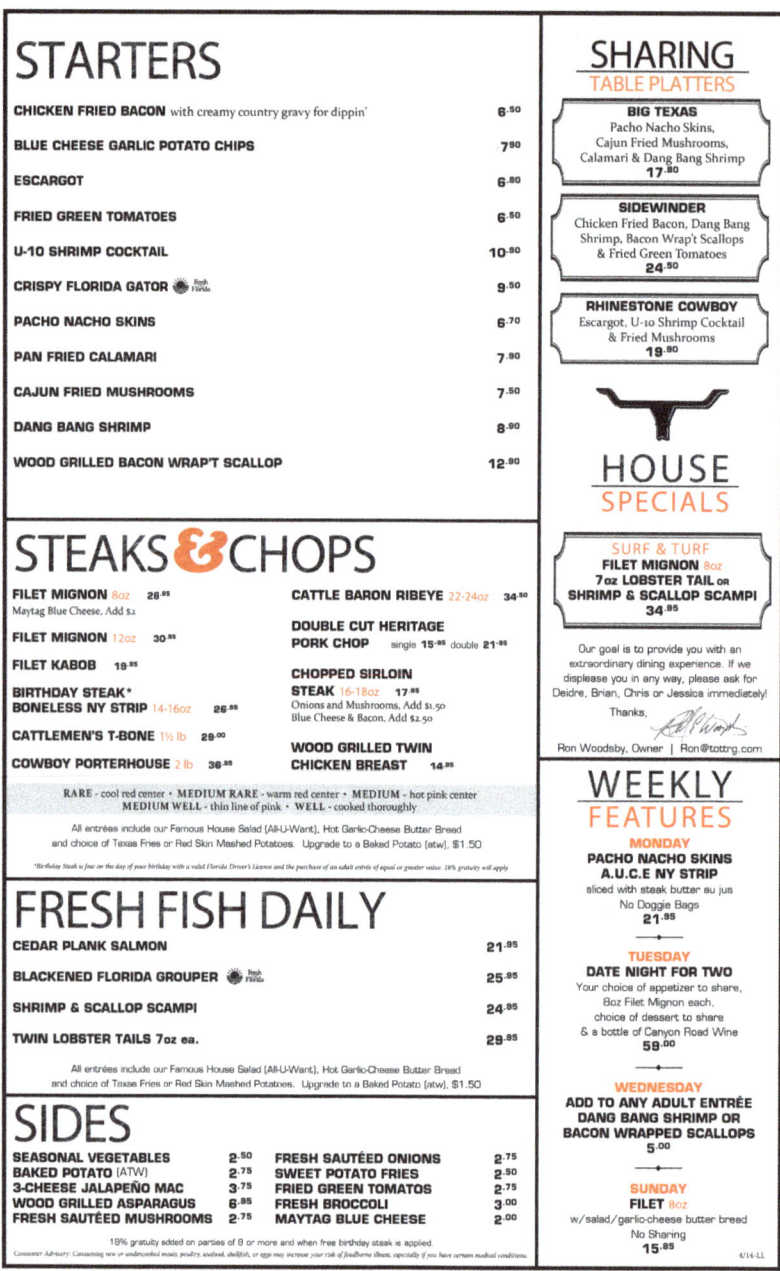

Innovative billboard in Lakeland, Florida

RESTAURANTS

TEXAS CATTLE COMPANY
St. Petersburg
Established 1985

RED LOBSTER...THE BEGINNING

STARTERS

CHICKEN FRIED BACON with creamy country gravy for dippin'	6.50
BLUE CHEESE GARLIC POTATO CHIPS	7.90
ESCARGOT	6.80
FRIED GREEN TOMATOES	6.50
U-10 SHRIMP COCKTAIL	10.90
CRISPY FLORIDA GATOR *Fresh Florida*	9.50
PACHO NACHO SKINS	6.70
PAN FRIED CALAMARI	7.90
CAJUN FRIED MUSHROOMS	7.50
DANG BANG SHRIMP	8.90
WOOD GRILLED BACON WRAP'T SCALLOP	12.90

STEAKS & CHOPS

FILET MIGNON 8oz 26.95
Maytag Blue Cheese, Add $2

FILET MIGNON 12oz 30.95

FILET KABOB 19.95

BIRTHDAY STEAK*
BONELESS NY STRIP 14-16oz 26.95

CATTLEMEN'S T-BONE 1½ lb 29.00

COWBOY PORTERHOUSE 2 lb 36.95

CATTLE BARON RIBEYE 22-24oz 34.90

DOUBLE CUT HERITAGE PORK CHOP single 15.95 double 21.95

CHOPPED SIRLOIN STEAK 16-18oz 17.95
Onions and Mushrooms, Add $1.50
Blue Cheese & Bacon, Add $2.50

WOOD GRILLED TWIN CHICKEN BREAST 14.95

RARE - cool red center • MEDIUM RARE - warm red center • MEDIUM - hot pink center
MEDIUM WELL - thin line of pink • WELL - cooked thoroughly

All entrées include our Famous House Salad (All-U-Want), Hot Garlic-Cheese Butter Bread
and choice of Texas Fries or Red Skin Mashed Potatoes. Upgrade to a Baked Potato (atw) $1.50

*Birthday Steak is free on the day of your birthday with a valid Florida Driver's License and the purchase of an adult entrée of equal or greater value. 18% gratuity will apply

FRESH FISH DAILY

CEDAR PLANK SALMON	21.95
BLACKENED FLORIDA GROUPER *Fresh Florida*	25.95
SHRIMP & SCALLOP SCAMPI	24.95
TWIN LOBSTER TAILS 7oz ea.	29.95

All entrées include our Famous House Salad (All-U-Want), Hot Garlic-Cheese Butter Bread
and choice of Texas Fries or Red Skin Mashed Potatoes. Upgrade to a Baked Potato (atw) $1.50

SIDES

SEASONAL VEGETABLES	2.50	**FRESH SAUTÉED ONIONS**	2.75
BAKED POTATO (ATW)	2.75	**SWEET POTATO FRIES**	2.50
3-CHEESE JALAPEÑO MAC	3.75	**FRIED GREEN TOMATOS**	2.75
WOOD GRILLED ASPARAGUS	6.95	**FRESH BROCCOLI**	3.00
FRESH SAUTÉED MUSHROOMS	2.75	**MAYTAG BLUE CHEESE**	2.00

18% gratuity added on parties of 8 or more and when free birthday steak is applied.
Consumer Advisory: Consuming raw or undercooked meats, poultry, seafood, shellfish, or eggs may increase your risk of foodborne illness, especially if you have certain medical conditions.

SHARING
TABLE PLATTERS

BIG TEXAS
Pacho Nacho Skins,
Cajun Fried Mushrooms,
Calamari & Dang Bang Shrimp
17.80

SIDEWINDER
Chicken Fried Bacon, Dang Bang
Shrimp, Bacon Wrap't Scallops
& Fried Green Tomatoes
24.50

RHINESTONE COWBOY
Escargot, U-10 Shrimp Cocktail
& Fried Mushrooms
19.90

HOUSE SPECIALS

SURF & TURF
FILET MIGNON 8oz
7oz LOBSTER TAIL OR
SHRIMP & SCALLOP SCAMPI
34.95

Our goal is to provide you with an extraordinary dining experience. If we displease you in any way, please ask for Deidre, Brian, Chris or Jessica immediately!

Thanks,

Ron Woodsby, Owner | Ron@tottrg.com

WEEKLY FEATURES

MONDAY
PACHO NACHO SKINS
A.U.C.E NY STRIP
sliced with steak butter au jus
No Doggie Bags
21.95

TUESDAY
DATE NIGHT FOR TWO
Your choice of appetizer to share,
8oz Filet Mignon each,
choice of dessert to share
& a bottle of Canyon Road Wine
59.00

WEDNESDAY
ADD TO ANY ADULT ENTRÉE
DANG BANG SHRIMP OR
BACON WRAPPED SCALLOPS
5.00

SUNDAY
FILET 8oz
w/ salad/garlic-cheese butter bread
No Sharing
15.85

4/14-LL

RESTAURANTS

CHARLEY'S STEAK HOUSE
Orange Blossom Trail
Established 1985

STEAK HOUSE

Since 1973

What Makes Us Different?

Each Steer is exclusively raised for us by Harris Ranch. "We know our Steers from the day they're born"

No Antibiotics • No Hormones • Humane Treatment

USDA Prime & Choice Angus - 3 year old maturity range "A"

Aged 32-48 days for "flavor and tenderness"

Hand-cut on premises "by our managers only!"

Seasoned with fine ground sea salt, pepper and other secret seasonings 24 hours in advance to allow the natural flavors to blend, develop and bloom

1200°
Cooked over Citrus & Oak wood fire in our custom built pits

Citrus wood is not readily available, so we cut our own

No Steakhouse in the Top Ten cooks this way! It's a lot of extra work!
We feel all this effort is what sets us apart.
Thank you for your business,

AWARD WINNING • CUSTOMER DRIVEN • QUALITY OBSESSED

  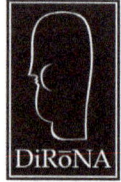  

Want to buy our steaks to cook on your grill - Ask your server!

RESTAURANTS

Appetizers

Beef Tenderloin Carpaccio	13.95
Seasoned Seared Tenderloin, Thinly Sliced and Drizzled with a Unique Creole Aioli, Topped with Aged Reggiano Parmesan	
Jumbo U-10 Shrimp Cocktail	10.95
Served Chilled with a Homemade Cocktail Sauce	
Langostinos	8.95
Succulent Deep Water Chilean Langostinos, Broiled in Pure Butter with Just a Hint of Garlic	
Shrimp & Scallop Scampi	12.95
Gulf Shrimp and Scallops Baked in Pure Butter, Garlic, Fresh Italian Parsley, Cognac & Parmesan Bread Crumbs	
Cedar Plank Roasted Crab Cakes	12.95
Jumbo Lump "Maryland Style" Crab Cakes	
Spicy Ahi Tuna Nachos	6.95
Tempura-Wasabi Nachos with Sushi Grade Ahi Tuna Tar-Tar	
Escargot Bourguignonne	8.95
Baked in Garlic Butter and served with Toasted Garlic Bread	
Cajun Gator Bites	7.95
1/3 Pound of Crispy Gator in Florida Citrus Marinade with Creamy Horseradish "Tiger" Sauce	
Bacon Wrapped Scallops	9.50
Sushi Grade Scallops with Applewood Smoked Bacon	
Seared Rare Tuna Sashimi Half 8.50 Full 15.95	
Served with Citrus Sesame, Ginger and Wasabi	
Pan Fried Calamari	10.95
Sautéed Fresh Red, Green and Yellow Peppers with Garlic and Scallions	
Cajun Fried Mushrooms	7.50
"A Platter to be Shared" Deep Fried in a Cajun Seasoned Flour	
Crispy Almond Fried Lobster	17.95
Caribbean Lobster, Almond Batter Fried to a golden brown, served with Orange Blossom-Honey Mustard sauce	
Charley's Shrimp Trio	16.95
Crispy Hand Breaded, Shrimp Cocktail & Shrimp Louis	

Key West Sampler
Pan Seared Calamari, Buttered Langostinos and Lump Crab Stuffed Shrimp "Scampi Style"
26.95

Seasonal Fresh Fish

We commit to purchasing only the freshest fish off the day boats. Due to our commitment to fresh seafood, all fresh fish is limited to availability. Our server will explain today's selections. Enjoy.

Oak Grilled - Blackened - Bronzed

Yellow Fin "Ahi" Tuna

Swordfish

Salmon

Pompano

Mahi-Mahi

Wahoo

Black Grouper

Red Grouper

Red Snapper

Sauces & Salsas

Lump Crab Beurre Blanc - 4.50
with Mushrooms & a Silky Lemon Butter Sauce

Fresh Pineapple Mango Salsa - 2.00
With Cilantro and Jalapeño

Oscar Style - 6.95
Alaskan King Crab with Grilled Asparagus and Hollandaise Sauce

Cajun Oscar Style - 7.50
Langostinos and Lump Crab with a Cajun Spiced Creamy Alfredo Sauce

Pesto Roast Garlic Butter - 3.00
with Basil and Roasted Garlic

Dill Cream Sauce - 2.00
with Red Onion and Parmesan

Hollandaise / Bearnaise - 2.50
"Classic Style"
Add Lump Crab - 3.00

From the Deep Blue Sea

All Entrées include our fresh green garden salad bar, Red Skin Garlic Mashed Potatoes or Charley's Hand Cut Steak Fries.
Charley's offers a Grilled Caesar Salad or Charley's Specialty Salad as a substitute for $2.95 with Entrée.

Australian Rock Lobster Tail (1 - 1 1/4 lb)	39.95
Tender Lobster Tail Delicately Prepared with Seasoned Breadcrumbs, Fresh Lemon, Drawn Butter and then Baked to Perfection. (each additional ounce over 1 1/4 lb, add $2.75)	
Alaskan King Crab (1-1/2 lbs.)	30.95
Succulent Red King Crab Served Cool with a Side of Drawn Butter.	
Stone Crab (2-1/4 lbs.)	In Season, October thru May
(In Season Only) Chilled Crabs Cracked and Served with Johnnie's Famous Mustard Sauce.	
Cedar Plank Salmon	21.95
Fresh Alaskan King Salmon, Plank Roasted over Citrus and Oak with a Parmesan-Red Onion Aioli Crust.	
Charley's Mixed Grill	28.95
Two Seasonal Fish Selections, White Large Gulf Shrimp, Jumbo Sea Scallops Sautéed in Butter, Garlic and White Wine	
Langostinos	18.95
Succulent Deep Water Chilean Langostinos, Broiled in Pure Butter with Just a Hint of Garlic. If you like Lobster, you'll love Langostinos.	
Jumbo Fried Shrimp	18.95
Our Jumbo Shrimp Hand Breaded To Order. Made Fresh when each Ticket enters the Kitchen.	
Planked Crab Cake & Fried Shrimp	19.95
Jumbo Lump "Maryland Style" Crab Cake Cedar Roasted and Our Famous Jumbo Hand Breaded Shrimp. The Perfect Combination	

To Complement your Entrée, may we suggest Charley's Bacon-Cheddar Smashed Potatoes, Parmesan Truffle Fries, or Sea Salt Baked Potato as a substitute for an additional $3.00.

There is a risk with consuming raw or undercooked proteins. If you have chronic illness of the stomach, liver, blood or have immune disorders you are at a greater risk of serious illness from consuming raw or undercooked proteins.

RED LOBSTER...THE BEGINNING

Charley's Signature Steaks
- On The Bone Steaks -

Why are they so much tastier?

The surrounding bone releases flavor during the cooking process, helps retain the meat's natural moisture and helps tenderize the steaks. Our in-house butchers leave precisely a 1/4 inch cap around the opposing side of the steak. Seasoned and then cooked over an 1,100 degree woodfire, giving you the best steak you have ever tasted. "Top Ten Status"

> All Entrées include Red Skin Garlic Mashed Potatoes or Charley's Hand-Cut Steak Fries, Charley's Signature Spinning Salad Bowl or Our Famous Fresh Salad Table including Signature Grilled Caesar; Beefsteak Tomato, Blue Cheese, Onion & Steakhouse Bacon Salad; & The Classic Wedge for an additional $2.95

Charley's Ultimate Surf and Turf (For Two) — 99.99
Double Cut 50oz Porterhouse and 1-1/4 Pound Lobster Tail

King of the Bone New York Strip 2 1/2" Thick — 32.95
Known for richness-coupled with Hand Turned Aging Process and Open Pit Cooking, produces the Juiciest of all Cuts.

Porterhouse (32 oz.) — 38.95
The Porterhouse is a Rich Flavored Well Aged Steak Best Suited for the Hearty Appetite.

Bone-in Ribeye Steak (24 oz.) — 36.95
Thick Cut Angus Ribeye aged and very rich due to the extensive marbling. (Blackened with Lump Crab, Langostinos & Cajun Alfredo Sauce, add $5.00)

T-Bone (20 oz.) — 26.95
The T-Bone has the same rich flavor as the Porterhouse, but with a smaller filet. Served bone-in, as the bone helps retain more of the natural juices.

Filet Mignon — 10oz - 29.95   14oz - 33.95
The Tenderest of all Steak Cuts is the Filet Mignon. We Select and Buy the Heaviest USDA Prime and Choice Western Grain-Fed Tenderloins and Age them for that Tender, Flavorful and Sweet Taste. (Stuffed with Bleu Cheese or Steakhouse Bacon Wrapped, add 2.50)

New York Strip Sirloin (18 oz.) — 28.95
This steak is called the New York Strip or Strip Sirloin, a Very Popular Steak because of its Flavor. We Serve the Strip Sirloin Boneless and Well-Trimmed. (Finished with La Bella Gorgonzola Fondue, add $5.00)

Tenderloin Brochette (While they last) — 16.95
Our Sirloin and Tenderloin Tips with Fresh Vegetables, Flame Broiled on a Skewer.

Chopped Steak (While they last) — 13.95
We use the Trimmings from our Prime and Choice Steaks and Grind them Fresh Daily to make our Chopped Steak. Served with Sauteed Mushrooms and Onions. (Add Melted Jacksbury, Swiss or Blue Cheese for $2.50)

All Entrées Can Surf
(Served with Adult Entrée Only)

Crab Crusted	Charley's Oscar	10oz Lobster Tail
topped with Lump Crab, Mushrooms, Buerre Blanc & Alaskan Crusher Claw	8.95	Broiled • Almond Fried • Stuffed
12.50		17.50 ea

Finishing Touches

Bearnaise Sauce	Au Poivre Peppercorn Sauce	Maytag Blue Cheese Crumbles
2.50	with Pepper Encrusting (optional)	2.50
Steakhouse Bacon	3.50	La Bella Gorgonzola Fondue
2.00 per slice		5.00

Chops • Chicken • Etc

Pork Chops (1-1/2" Thick) — Single Chop - 13.95   Double Chops - 17.95
We take the Same Pride in our Pork Chops as we do in our Steaks, serving you only Chops, which have never been frozen, seasoned with Fresh Herbs and Lemon Juice, grilled over our Natural Wood-Burning pit to a Juicy and Tender Perfection.

Flame-Broiled Chicken — 12.95
Two Moist and Juicy Chicken Breasts, Marinated with Sweet Butter, a touch of Lemon, cooked on the Open Fire the way the Indians used to Cook. We think you'll Appreciate the Difference in our Chicken.

Flame-Broiled Chicken and Pork Chops — 15.95
Cooked over our natural wood-burning pit.

> RARE . . . Brown-Seared Crust with a Cool Red Center
> MEDIUM RARE . . . Brown-Seared Crust with a Warm Red Center
> MEDIUM . . . Outside of Steak Well Done, Dark Brown with a Hot Pink Center
> MEDIUM WELL . . . Outside Dark Brown, Inside Done with a Thin Line of Pink in the Center, But Still Juicy
> WELL . . . Outside Dark Brown, Center Cooked Thoroughly
> PLEASE ALLOW ADDITIONAL TIME FOR STEAKS COOKED MEDIUM WELL OR WELL
> TOTALLY RESPONSIBLE FOR STEAKS COOKED WELL DONE (IF BUTTERFLIED)

Side Orders

Charley's Smashed Potatoes		Sauteed Mushrooms & Onions	6.95	Cajun Fried Mushrooms	7.95
Bacon-Cheddar Mashed	5.95	Fresh Oak-Grilled Vegetables	5.95	ATW Giant Baked Potato	x.xx
Traditional	3.00			Parmesan Truffle Fries	5.95
Gorgonzola Fondue with Steakhouse Bacon	7.95	Twice Baked Sweet Potato with Cinnamon Butter & Brown Sugar	3.95	Fresh Baked Garlic Bread	2.75
Creamy Au Poivre Peppercorn Sauce	5.95	Chef's Spinach Artichoke Casserole For Two	6.95	Woodfired Jalapeño & Cheddar Hash	x.xx
				Jumbo Fresh Asparagus Milanaise with Bearnaise	6.95

Gift Certificates Available • 17% on Birthday Parties and Parties of 6 or More • Please - No Separate Checks on Parties of Six or More

RESTAURANTS

MMVIII

2008 AMERICA'S TOP TEN
STEAKHOUSES

Tom Horan's America's Top Ten Club is proud to name our list of America's Top Ten Steakhouses* for 2008:

1. **CHARLEY'S STEAK HOUSE**
   Orlando, Florida
2. **DICKIE BRENNAN'S STEAKHOUSE**
   New Orleans, Louisiana
3. **PLAZA III, THE STEAKHOUSE**
   Kansas City, Missouri
4. **AL BIERNAT'S**
   Dallas, Texas
5. **E.B. GREEN'S STEAKHOUSE**
   Buffalo, New York
6. **AJ MAXWELL'S STEAKHOUSE**
   New York, New York
7. **VIC & ANTHONY'S**
   Houston, Texas
8. **MALONE'S**
   Lexington, Kentucky
9. **ELWAY'S**
   Denver, Colorado
10. **KEVIN RATHBUN STEAK**
    Atlanta, Georgia

*Non-chain establishments

AMERICA'S TOP TEN CLUB MEMBERSHIP

An excellent opportunity to show your support and recognize quality dining is to become a member of America's Top Ten Club. We invite you to join America's Top Ten Club as an associate food critic and a member. Please mail your check for twenty five dollars to: Tom Horan's America's Top Ten Club, 12 Greenway Plaza, Suite 1100, Houston, Texas 77046 or go to www.tomhoran.com.

RED LOBSTER...THE BEGINNING

CHARLEY'S STEAK HOUSE
Celebration
Established 1988

RESTAURANTS

Appetizers

Seared Rare Tuna Sashimi* — 13.50
Served with citrus, sesame, ginger and wasabi.

Florida Stone Crab Claws (Fresh Florida) — MKT
Chilled claws cracked and served with mustard sauce, just like "Johnnie's made them famous."

Colossal U-10 Shrimp Cocktail — 12.95
Served icy cold with a housemade cocktail, remoulade & classic Louis sauce.

Escargot Bourgogne — 8.95
Baked in garlic butter and served with toasted bread for your dipping pleasure. Yum!

Blue Cheese Kettle Fries — 7.95
Crispy fries tossed in parmesan, garlic and Maytag blue cheese. Served with horseradish cream.

Lobster Bisque — 8.95
Rich and creamy bisque bursting with Maine lobster and finished tableside with fine sherry.

Bacon Wrapped "Sushi Grade" Scallops — 11.95
Diver-caught scallops with Applewood smoked bacon.

Jumbo Fried Shrimp — 10.95
Jumbo Key West Pink Shrimp, hand-breaded to order and fried golden brown. Served with housemade cocktail sauce.

Florida Gator (Fresh Florida) — 8.50
A unique Florida taste treat. 1/3 pound of citrus marinated gator, crispy fried and served with a slightly sweet & tangy horseradish aioli.

Scallop Gratinaise Stuffed Shrimp — 9.50
Colossal U-10 shrimp stuffed with sweet Cape May scallops broiled in pure butter, fresh lemon and topped with toasted sherry breadcrumbs.

Pan Fried Calamari — 10.95
Sautéed with a red, yellow and green assortment of banana, cherry and bell peppers.

Wagyu Beef Sashimi "Hot Rock"* . . . 15.95
You sear tableside on a hot volcanic stone. Served with Himalayan sea salt, mushroom chips, truffle mayo and a light citrus-soy ponzu.

Market Fresh Fish

All entrées served with Charley's signature house salad and garlic-cheese butter bread.

Blackened Gulf Grouper (Fresh Florida) — 29.95
Seared on a cast iron skillet with cajun spices, finished with Key Lime butter and pineapple-mango salsa.

Ahi Asian Cajun Tuna Mignon — 32.95
Spicy cajun seasoned Ahi tuna encrusted in wasabi-nori crisps and seared rare with a citrus soy Asian BBQ vinaigrette. Served atop wasabi mashed potatoes.

Cedar Plank Roasted Salmon — 27.95
Atlantic King Salmon topped with a light parmesan red onion aioli and cedar plank roasted over our custom citrus wood burning pit.

Lobster Mixed Grill — 35.95
1/2 pound stuffed lobster tail, Applewood bacon wrapped "sushi grade" scallops, cedar plank roasted salmon and two colossal U-10 shrimp topped with jumbo lump crab and beurre blanc.

Charley's Steak House is proud to serve sustainable, wild caught and responsibly farmed fish and seafood.

From the Deep Blue Sea

All entrées served with Charley's signature house salad and garlic-cheese butter bread.

Australian Rock Lobster Tail (1 - 1¼ lbs) — add $2.75 per ounce for larger sizes . . . 54.50
Tender lobster tail delicately prepared with seasoned breadcrumbs, fresh lemon, drawn butter and then baked to perfection. Ask your server for larger available sizes.

Bering Strait King Crab — 1 lb - 42.95
Alaska's sweetest gift! Red King Crab served hot with lemon and drawn butter or cold with housemade cocktail sauce and horseradish.

Florida Stone Crab (2¼ lbs) (Fresh Florida) — MKT
In Season Only. Chilled claws cracked and served with Johnnie's famous mustard sauce.

Fried Gulf Shrimp (Colossal U-10) — 25.95
U-10 shrimp hand breaded to order only. Made fresh when each ticket enters the kitchen.

Think Globally
- Act Locally -
Dress Casually

Children's
- Menu -
Available

Aged Steaks
- Shipped -
Continental U.S.

Charley's Apparel and
- Steak Knives are -
Available!

1200°F

Aged 32 to 48 Days • Hand Cut Daily By Management
Cooked Over Citrus & Oak Log Fire
No Antibiotics • Hormone Free

RARE	Brown-Seared Crust with a Cool Red Center
PITTSBURGH	Charred Crust, Cool Red Center
MEDIUM RARE	Brown-Seared Crust with a Warm Red Center
MEDIUM	Outside of Steak Well Done, Dark Brown with a Hot Pink Center
MEDIUM WELL	Outside Dark Brown, Inside Done with a Thin Line of Pink in the Center, But Still Juicy
WELL (Allow 20 mins)	Outside Dark Brown, Center Cooked Thoroughly

TOTALLY RESPONSIBLE FOR STEAKS COOKED WELL DONE (IF BUTTERFLIED)

All Entrées can Surf
Served with Adult Entrée Only!

Classic Style Oscar
Alaskan King Crab, Grilled Asparagus and Hollandaise
7.95

Colossal Shrimp
Two U-10 Shrimp
w/ Jumbo Lump Crab & Buerre Blanc
8.50

½ lb Stuffed Lobster Tail
Stuffed with
Cape May Scallop Gratinaise
12.95

All entrées served with Charley's signature house salad and garlic-cheese butter bread.

King of the Bone
2 ½" Thick New York Strip known for richness, coupled with our hand-turned aging process and open pit cooking, produces the juiciest of all cuts.
55.95

Twin Stuffed Lobster Tails
Two half pound Florida lobster tails stuffed with sweet Cape May scallops broiled in pure butter, fresh lemon and topped with toasted breadcrumbs.
39.95

Share the Above - "The Ultimate Surf & Turf for Two"
39.95 per person

Kansas City Strip (Bone-In 22 oz.) — 32.95
Known for its richness, coupled with our hand-turned aging process and open pit cooking produces the juiciest of steaks! (with creamy Cognac-cracked pepper sauce, add $2.50)

Filet Mignon — 8oz - 34.95   12oz - 42.95
The filet mignon is the tenderest of all cuts . . . . . Oscar style, add $6.95
Maytag bleu cheese stuffed, add $3
Bacon wrapped, add $2

Heritage Ribeyes

Blue Creek Bison Ribeye
Naturally lean, lower in fat, higher in protein than normal beef.
54.95

Angus Bone-in Ribeye
100% USDA Prime, heavily marbled.
Aged 4-6 weeks.
42.95

Wagyu / "Kobe Style"
The caviar of all ribeyes. Eats like butter.
From Greg Norman's Ranch.
64.95

Pork Chops (1½" Thick) Add (2) jumbo fried shrimp $5.50   Single Chop - 18.95   Double Chops - 23.95
We take the same pride in our pork chops as we do in our steaks, serving you only chops which have never been frozen, seasoned with fresh herbs and lemon juice, grilled over our natural wood-burning pit to a juicy and tender perfection.

Flame-Broiled Chicken — 15.95
Two moist and juicy chicken breasts, marinated with sweet butter, a touch of lemon, cooked on the open fire the way the Indians used to cook.
Colossal shrimp with lump crab & buerre blanc, add $5.50

Finishing Touches

Steakhouse Bacon Lardons 2.50	Sautéed Mushrooms 3.50	Hollandaise / Béarnaise Sauce 2.50
Maytag Blue Cheese Crumbles Delicious on your salad, steak or potato 2.75	Sautéed Onions 3.00	Creamy Cognac-Cracked Pepper Sauce 2.50

Potatoes • Vegetables • Sides

Lobster Macaroni & Cheese	14.50	Fried Green Tomatoes	5.95	Roast Garlic Red Skin Mashed	5.95
Steamed Broccoli Lemon, Garlic and E.V.O.O.	5.95	Oak-Grilled Vegetables	5.95	Steakhouse Bacon & Cheddar Mashed	6.95
		Black Pepper Parmesan Kettle Fries	5.95	AuGratin Potatoes	4.95
Jumbo Fresh Asparagus with Hollandaise	5.95	Creamed Spinach	5.95	Sea Salt Baked Potato (ATW) with Bacon, Sour Cream & Tillamook Cheddar	4.95

On & Off Site - Catering - From 75 to 3000 People	Gift - Cards - Available	17% Gratuity - on Parties of - Six or More	Private - Function - Dining Rooms

RESTAURANTS

Charley's
STEAK HOUSE
& Seafood Grille

Prime Time
Top 10 Steakhouse of America
2003 - 2013

Best of Award of Excellence
Wine Spectator Magazine
1995 - 2013

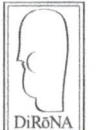
DiRōNA Award
Distinguished Restaurants of North America
2003 - 2013

Beef Backer Award
International Council of Beef
1997 - 1998

America's Top Ten Steakhouse
Tom Horan's America's Top Ten Club
#1- 2007 - 2012 (1995 - 2012)

Epicurean Award
2006 - 2013

Santé Restaurant Award
Culinary • Wine • Service • Spirits
Santé Magazine
2007 - 2011

Award of Unique Distinction
Wine Enthusiast Magazine
2006 - 2011

Golden Palm Award
Orlando Magazine
1997

Survey Rated Excellent

Diamond Wine Award
International Award of Excellence
2001-2007

Golden Service Crown
Excelsior Business Club
2007 - 2009

"Best Steak House" in Orlando
Orlando Magazine
1997 - 1998, 2002, 2010 - 2013

International Award of Excellence
Top 10 Steakhouse, Top 25 Overall
2004

Golden Cup Award
Specialty Coffee Association of America
1998, 2001 - 2013

Orlando • Celebration • Tampa

2901 Parkway Boulevard • Kissimmee, Florida 34747
Telephone 407.396.6055
www.CharleysSteakHouse.com

Lakeland
St. Petersburg

Orlando

Orlando

Johnnie's HIDEAWAY
Lake Buena Vista

Orlando
Lake Mary

*There is a risk with consuming raw or undercooked proteins. If you have chronic illness of the stomach, liver, blood or have immune disorders you are at a greater risk of serious illness from consuming raw or undercooked proteins.

CHARLEY'S STEAK HOUSE
International Drive
Established 1992

RESTAURANTS

Appetizers

Seared Rare Tuna Sashimi* — 13.50
Served with citrus, sesame, ginger and wasabi.

Florida Stone Crab Claws (Fresh Florida) — MKT
Chilled claws cracked and served with mustard sauce, just like "Johnnie's made them famous."

Colossal U-10 Shrimp Cocktail — 12.95
Served icy cold with a housemade cocktail, remoulade & classic Louis sauce.

Escargot Bourgogne — 8.95
Baked in garlic butter and served with toasted bread for your dipping pleasure. Yum!

Blue Cheese Kettle Fries — 7.95
Crispy fries tossed in parmesan, garlic and Maytag blue cheese. Served with horseradish cream.

Lobster Bisque — 8.95
Rich and creamy bisque bursting with Maine lobster and finished tableside with fine sherry.

Bacon Wrapped "Sushi Grade" Scallops — 11.95
Diver-caught scallops with Applewood smoked bacon.

Jumbo Fried Shrimp — 10.95
Jumbo Key West Pink Shrimp, hand-breaded to order and fried golden brown. Served with housemade cocktail sauce.

Florida Gator (Fresh Florida) — 8.50
A unique Florida taste treat. 1/3 pound of citrus marinated gator, crispy fried and served with a slightly sweet & tangy horseradish aioli.

Scallop Gratinaise Stuffed Shrimp — 9.50
Colossal U-10 shrimp stuffed with sweet Cape May scallops broiled in pure butter, fresh lemon and topped with toasted sherry breadcrumbs.

Pan Fried Calamari — 10.95
Sautéed with a red, yellow and green assortment of banana, cherry and bell peppers.

Wagyu Beef Sashimi "Hot Rock"* . . . 15.95
You sear tableside on a hot volcanic stone. Served with Himalayan sea salt, mushroom chips, truffle mayo and a light citrus-soy ponzu.

Market Fresh Fish

All entrées served with Charley's signature house salad and garlic-cheese butter bread.

Blackened Gulf Grouper (Fresh Florida) — 29.95
Seared on a cast iron skillet with cajun spices, finished with Key Lime butter and pineapple-mango salsa.

Ahi Asian Cajun Tuna Mignon — 32.95
Spicy cajun seasoned Ahi tuna encrusted in wasabi-nori crisps and seared rare with a citrus soy Asian BBQ vinaigrette. Served atop wasabi mashed potatoes.

Cedar Plank Roasted Salmon — 27.95
Atlantic King Salmon topped with a light parmesan red onion aioli and cedar plank roasted over our custom citrus wood burning pit.

Lobster Mixed Grill — 35.95
1/2 pound stuffed lobster tail, Applewood bacon wrapped "sushi grade" scallops, cedar plank roasted salmon and two colossal U-10 shrimp topped with jumbo lump crab and buerre blanc.

⊱ Charley's Steak House is proud to serve sustainable, wild caught and responsibly farmed fish and seafood. ⊰

From the Deep Blue Sea

All entrées served with Charley's signature house salad and garlic-cheese butter bread.

Australian Rock Lobster Tail (1 - 1¼ lbs) — add $2.75 per ounce for larger sizes . . . 54.50
Tender lobster tail delicately prepared with seasoned breadcrumbs, fresh lemon, drawn butter and then baked to perfection. Ask your server for larger available sizes.

Bering Strait King Crab — 1 lb - 42.95
Alaska's sweetest gift! Red King Crab served hot with lemon and drawn butter or cold with housemade cocktail sauce and horseradish.

Florida Stone Crab (2¼ lbs) (Fresh Florida) — MKT
In Season Only. Chilled claws cracked and served with Johnnie's famous mustard sauce.

Fried Gulf Shrimp (Colossal U-10) — 25.95
U-10 shrimp hand breaded to order only. Made fresh when each ticket enters the kitchen.

Think Globally
- Act Locally -
Dress Casually

Children's
- Menu -
Available

Aged Steaks
- Shipped -
Continental U.S.

Charley's Apparel and
- Steak Knives are -
Available!

RED LOBSTER...THE BEGINNING

1200°F

Aged 32 to 48 Days • Hand Cut Daily By Management
Cooked Over Citrus & Oak Log Fire
No Antibiotics • Hormone Free

RARE	Brown-Seared Crust with a Cool Red Center
PITTSBURGH	Charred Crust, Cool Red Center
MEDIUM RARE	Brown-Seared Crust with a Warm Red Center
MEDIUM	Outside of Steak Well Done, Dark Brown with a Hot Pink Center
MEDIUM WELL	Outside Dark Brown, Inside Done with a Thin Line of Pink in the Center, But Still Juicy
WELL (Allow 20 mins)	Outside Dark Brown, Center Cooked Thoroughly

TOTALLY RESPONSIBLE FOR STEAKS COOKED WELL DONE (IF BUTTERFLIED)

All Entrées can Surf
Served with Adult Entrée Only!

Classic Style Oscar
Alaskan King Crab, Grilled Asparagus and Hollandaise
7.95

Colossal Shrimp
Two U-10 Shrimp
w/ Jumbo Lump Crab & Buerre Blanc
8.50

½ lb Stuffed Lobster Tail
Stuffed with
Cape May Scallop Gratinaise
12.95

All entrées served with Charley's signature house salad and garlic-cheese butter bread.

King of the Bone
2 ½" Thick New York Strip known for richness, coupled with our hand-turned aging process and open pit cooking, produces the juiciest of all cuts.
55.95

Twin Stuffed Lobster Tails
Two half pound Florida lobster tails stuffed with sweet Cape May scallops broiled in pure butter, fresh lemon and topped with toasted breadcrumbs.
39.95

> **Share the Above** - "The Ultimate Surf & Turf for Two"
> 39.95 per person

Kansas City Strip (Bone-In 22 oz.) — 32.95
Known for its richness, coupled with our hand-turned aging process and open pit cooking produces the juiciest of steaks! (with creamy Cognac-cracked pepper sauce, add $2.50)

Filet Mignon — 8oz - 34.95   12oz - 42.95
The filet mignon is the tenderest of all cuts . . . . . Oscar style, add $6.95
Maytag bleu cheese stuffed, add $3
Bacon wrapped, add $2

Heritage Ribeyes

Blue Creek Bison Ribeye
Naturally lean, lower in fat, higher in protein than normal beef.
54.95

Angus Bone-in Ribeye
100% USDA Prime, heavily marbled.
Aged 4-6 weeks.
42.95

Wagyu / "Kobe Style"
The caviar of all ribeyes. Eats like butter.
From Greg Norman's Ranch.
64.95

Pork Chops (1½" Thick) Add (3) U-10 bacon wrapped shrimp $5.50   **Single Chop - 18.95**   **Double Chops - 23.95**
We take the same pride in our pork chops as we do in our steaks, serving you only chops which have never been frozen, seasoned with fresh herbs and lemon juice, grilled over our natural wood-burning pit to a juicy and tender perfection.

Flame-Broiled Chicken — 15.95
Two moist and juicy chicken breasts, marinated with sweet butter, a touch of lemon, cooked on the open fire the way the Indians used to cook.
Colossal shrimp with lump crab & buerre blanc, add $5.50

Finishing Touches

Steakhouse Bacon Lardons 2.50	Sautéed Mushrooms 3.50	Hollandaise / Béarnaise Sauce 2.50
Maytag Blue Cheese Crumbles Delicious on your salad, steak or potato 2.75	Sautéed Onions 3.00	Creamy Cognac-Cracked Pepper Sauce 2.50

Potatoes • Vegetables • Sides

Lobster Macaroni & Cheese	14.50	Fried Green Tomatoes	5.95	Roast Garlic Red Skin Mashed	5.95
		Oak-Grilled Vegetables	5.95	Steakhouse Bacon & Cheddar Mashed	6.95
Steamed Broccoli Lemon, Garlic and E.V.O.O.	5.95	Black Pepper Parmesan Kettle Fries	5.95	AuGratin Potatoes	4.95
Jumbo Fresh Asparagus with Hollandaise	5.95	Creamed Spinach	5.95	Sea Salt Baked Potato (ATW) with Bacon, Sour Cream & Tillamook Cheddar	4.95

On & Off Site
- Catering -
From 75 to 3000 People

Gift
- Cards -
Available

18% Gratuity
- on Parties of -
Six or More

Private
- Function -
Dining Rooms

RESTAURANTS

"Award Winning"
Charley's STEAK HOUSE

Prime Time
Top 10 Steakhouse of America
2003 - 2013

Best of Award of Excellence
Wine Spectator Magazine
1995 - 2013

DiRōNA Award
Distinguished Restaurants of North America
2003 - 2013

Beef Backer Award
International Council of Beef
1997 - 1998

America's Top Ten Steakhouse
Tom Horan's America's Top Ten Club
#1- 2007 - 2012 (1995 - 2012)

Epicurean Award
2006 - 2011

Santé Restaurant Award
Culinary • Wine • Service • Spirits
Santé Magazine
2007 - 2011

Award of Unique Distinction
Wine Enthusiast Magazine
2006 - 2011

Golden Palm Award
Orlando Magazine
1997

Survey Rated Excellent

Diamond Wine Award
International Award of Excellence
2001-2007

Golden Service Crown
Excelsior Business Club
2007 - 2009

"Best Steak House" in Orlando
Orlando Magazine
1997 - 1998, 2002, 2010 - 2013

International Award of Excellence
Top 10 Steakhouse, Top 25 Overall
2004

Golden Cup Award
Specialty Coffee Association of America
1998, 2001 - 2013

Orlando • Celebration • Tampa

8255 International Drive, Suite 100 • Orlando, FL 32819
Telephone 407.363.0228
www.CharleysSteakHouse.com

Lakeland
St. Petersburg

Orlando

Lake Buena Vista

Orlando

Orlando
Lake Mary

*There is a risk with consuming raw or uncooked proteins. If you have chronic illness of the stomach, liver, blood or have immune disorders you are at a greater risk of serious illness from consuming raw or undercooked proteins.

RED LOBSTER...THE BEGINNING

FISHBONES
Sand Lake Road
Established 1994

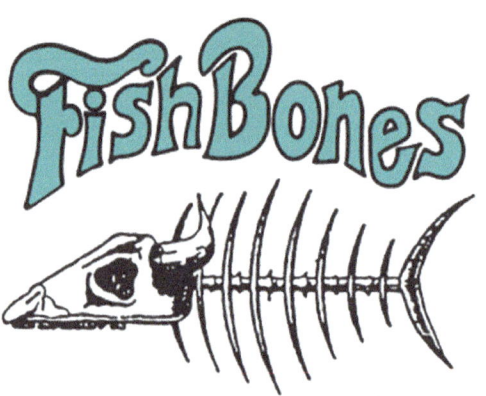

RESTAURANTS

MMVIII
2008 AMERICA'S TOP TEN HALL OF FAME
SEAFOOD HOUSES

Tom Horan's America's Top Ten Club is proud to honor the Best of the Best® for 2008

COMMANDER'S PALACE
New Orleans, Louisiana

FARALLON
San Francisco, California

FISHBONES
Orlando, Florida

GRAND CENTRAL OYSTER BAR
New York, New York

JAKE'S FAMOUS CRAWFISH
Portland, Oregon

JOE'S STONE CRAB
Miami Beach, Florida

THE OCEANAIRE
Minneapolis, Minnesota

WILLIE G'S SEAFOOD & STEAK HOUSE
Houston, Texas

Named in alphabetical order

RED LOBSTER...THE BEGINNING

STARTERS

Key West Shrimp Cocktail *Fresh Florida* 10.95
Key West Pink Shrimp with Key Lime juice, avocado, Bermuda onions. Served with crispy plaintain chips.

Florida Stone Crab Claws (In Season Only) *Fresh Florida* ....Market Price
1/2 pound of medium claws served cracked with Johnnie's famous mustard sauce.

New England Clam Chowder .... cup 3.25 .... bowl 4.50
Rich and creamy chowder with Cedar Key middleneck clams.

Yellow-fin Tuna Toro Wonton 12.95
Blend of tuna toro, sesame oil, Japanese masago. Served on a crunchy wonton with wasabi vinaigrette.

Florida Gator *Fresh Florida* 8.95
#1 grade Florida alligator tail lightly cajun breaded and fried. Served with horseradish aioli.

Escargot 7.95
Baked in fresh butter, garlic, cognac & parsley. Served with garlic bread.

Bahamian Smoked Fish Dip 7.95
Lightly smoked fresh catch, island spiced with a squeeze of lemon.

Blue Chips 7.95
Homemade blue cheese crema topped potato chips. You can't eat just one!

Crispy Almond Fried Lobster Tail 15.95
Served with orange blossom honey mustard.

Flash Fried Calamari 10.95
Flash fried calamari tossed with a sauteed assortment of red, yellow & green, banana, cherry & bell peppers. Served with cocktail sauce.

Frozen Strawberry Daiquiri

A frozen blend of Cruzan Light Rum and luscious fresh strawberries. (Some of us really know how to live!)

6.95

The Gulp of Mexico

Light up your night with a flaming Blue Sauza Conmemorativo Margarita. (Hold it with two hands!)

9.95

RESTAURANTS

FISH

Jumbo Fried Shrimp .... 8 shrimp 17.95
Our extra jumbo shrimp are hand breaded to order only.
Made fresh when each ticket enters the kitchen.

All-U-Can Eat Jumbo Shrimp 24.95
Same as above except you decide when to say enough is enough!
No sharing, please. No doggie bags.

Stuffed Shrimp 26.95
Jumbo shrimp stuffed with blue lump crab and finished with lemon buerre blanc.

Shrimp & Scallop Scampi 24.95
Jumbo shrimp and jumbo Cape May scallops baked in pure butter, garlic, fresh parsley,
cognac and parmesan herb bread crumbs.

Seasonal Crab Feature .... Market Price
Our fishmonger will only choose crab in the height of season. Depending on the time
of the year, these crabs may come from the shores of Maryland, the North Pacific
or the pristine waters of Florida.

Twin Lobster Tails 39.95
Two 7oz cold water lobster tails prepared your choice of broiled with lemon drawn butter
or almond fried with orange blossom honey.

FISH OF THE DAY
See Chef Michael's Daily Features
for Today's Fresh Catch and Preparations

HOUSE SPECIALTIES

Pork Chops .... single 17.95 .... double 23.95
We take the same pride in our pork chops as in our steaks. Serving you chops
which have never been frozen. These chops are cooked over our natural wood-burning
pit and are seasoned with fresh spices and lemon to keep them moist, juicy
and to accent the smoke flavor from the wood.

Grilled T-Bone Lamb Chops (1 ½" Thick) 27.95
5 chops cooked over a combination of citrus and oak wood in our special pit and served with
fresh mint sauce tableside.

Florida Orange Duck *Fresh Florida* 21.95
Fresh duck slow roasted to a crispy finish and topped with an orange-pepper sauce.

Flame Broiled Chicken Breast 15.95
Moist and juicy chicken breast marinated with sweet butter and lemon, then broiled
over the open fire the way the Indians used to cook. We think you'll appreciate the
difference in our chicken.

All entrées include garlic-cheese butter bread, special house salad
and your choice of red skin garlic mashed, cajun parmesan fries, glazed fresh vegetables or orzo pasta.
Or substitue your side for a baked potato ATW, add $2

RED LOBSTER...THE BEGINNING

BONES

Filet Mignon..8oz 32.95 ....12oz 36.95
The tenderest of all steak cuts. We select and buy the heaviest USDA Prime and Choice Western grain-fed tenderloins, and properly age them for that tender, flavorful and sweet taste.
Topped with melted gorgonzola cheese ... Add $2

New York Strip 17-18oz Boneless 29.95
1 ¾-2" Thick USDA choice strip aged six weeks on the premises, trimmed
within 1/8" for maximum flavor.

Bone-In Ribeye 24oz 36.95
Rich & extremely flavorful. Served well marbled. Do not order if you want a lean cut of beef.

served with your choice of teriyaki truffle butter, bearnaise or wood-roasted portabellas

---

PRIME RIB

Our prime rib is slow roasted for 23 hours in our specially-built oven using citrus and oak woods.
The cooking procedure will provide the most tender, juicy prime rib possible.
Served with au jus and horseradish sauce. Roasted fresh daily while they last.
Sorry, only two end cuts per roast.

Prime Rib of Beef - 12oz	Prime Rib of Beef - 16oz
24.95	28.95

Properly aged to ensure flavor. Served with au jus and horseradish sauce

---

Rare - cool red center • **Medium Rare** - warm red center • **Medium** - hot pink center
Medium Well - thin line of pink • **Well** - cooked thoroughly

COMBINATIONS

Grilled Chicken & Fried Shrimp 19.95
Citrus & oak grilled, skinless chicken breast served with five large golden brown fried shrimp.

Filet Mignon & ½ Almond Fried Lobster Tail...34.95
Our tender 8oz filet mignon and a ½ almond fried lobster tail.

Mixed Grill 29.95
Two select fresh fish of the day (chef's choice) served with our shrimp and scallop scampi.

*All entrées include garlic-cheese butter bread, special house salad
and your choice of red skin garlic mashed, cajun parmesan fries, glazed fresh vegetables or orzo pasta.
Or substitue your side for a baked potato ATW, add $2*

SIDES ~ TOPPINGS

Garlic Bread............................	2.25	Wood Grilled Asparagus......................	6.95
Sautéed Mushrooms............................	3.25	House Salad...	5.00
Baked Potato ATW................................	4.95	Oscar Topping......................................	9.25
with bacon, sour cream & Tillamook cheddar			
Cajun Parmesan Fries............................	2.75	Gorgonzola Cheese Crumbles..............	2.00
Fresh Vegetables...................................	2.75	Great on your steak or baked potato	

Consumer advisory: Consuming raw or uncooked meats, poultry, seafood, shellfish, or eggs may increase your risk of foodborne illness, especially if you have certain medical conditions.

RESTAURANTS

AFTER DINNER-COFFEE-ETC.

Fresh Ground Coffee

House Blend 2.95

Decaf 2.95

Espresso 3.75

Cappuccino 4.50

1952 Original Irish Coffee 6
Jameson, coffee, heavy cream & sugared rim

Cinnamon Delight 6
Kahlúa Cinnamon Spice, Chambord, cinnamon sugared rim & a cinnamon stick

FishBones' Signature Coffee 6
Bailey's Irish Cream, DeKuyper Amaretto & DeKuyper Crème de Cocoa

BEVERAGES

Bigelow Assorted Hot Teas 2.95

Orange Pekoe Fresh Brewed Iced Tea .. 2.95

Sodas 2.95
Pepsi, Diet Pepsi, Sierra Mist, Mt Dew, Ginger Ale, Dr. Pepper

IBC Root Beer 3.50

Bottled Water (Liter) 4.95
Acqua Panna, San Pellegrino

Milk 2.95

Juice 2.95
Orange, Cranberry

Fresh Made Lemonade 3.50

FRESH EXECUTION COCKTAILS

Cucumber Spice $9
Absolut Vodka, Freshly Squeezed Lime Juice, Fresh Cilantro, Cucumber, Serrano Peppers

Spiked Strawberry Basil Lemonade $11
Grey Goose Citron Vodka, Freshly Squeezed Lemonade, Strawberries, Basil

Sparkling Pears $9
Absolut Pears Vodka, St. Germain, Sage, La Marca Prosecco

The Hive $9
Plymouth Gin, Yuzu Juice, Orange Blossom Honey, Mint, Bitters

Strawberry Jam Mojito $9
Bacardi Rum, Freshly Squeezed Lime Juice, Fresh Mint, Coco Lopez Crème of Coconut

FishBones Signature Margarita $10
Herradura Tequila, Agave Nectar, Freshly Squeezed Lime Juice, Wasabi, Thai Basil

Gentleman Black Smash $11
Gentleman Jack Whiskey, Freshly Squeezed Lemon Juice, Blackberries, Mint

Açai Smash $9
VeeV Açai Spirit, Agave Nectar, Fresh Lemon Juice, Blueberries, Fresh Mint

CHARLEY'S STEAK HOUSE
Tampa
Established 1998

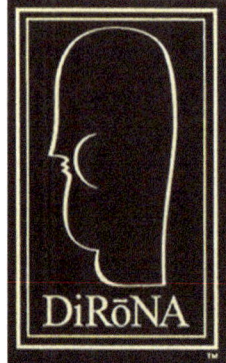   

RESTAURANTS

Tampa's Most Award-Winning Steakhouse

Prime Time
Top 10 Steakhouse of America
2003 - 2013

Best of Award of Excellence
Wine Spectator Magazine
1995 - 2013

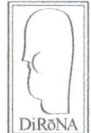
DiRōNA Award
Distinguished Restaurants of North America
2003 - 2013

Beef Backer Award
International Council of Beef
1997 - 1998

America's Top Ten Steakhouse
Tom Horan's America's Top Ten Club
#1- 2007 - 2012 (1995 - 2012)

Epicurean Award
2006 - 2011

Santé Restaurant Award
Culinary • Wine • Service • Spirits
Santé Magazine
2007 - 2010

Award of Unique Distinction
Wine Enthusiast Magazine
2006 - 2010

Golden Palm Award
Orlando Magazine
1997

Survey Rated Excellent

Diamond Wine Award
International Award of Excellence
2001-2007

Golden Service Crown
Excelsior Business Club
2007 - 2009

"Best Steak House" in Orlando
Orlando Magazine
1997 - 1998, 2002, 2010 - 2013

International Award of Excellence
Top 10 Steakhouse, Top 25 Overall
2004

Golden Cup Award
Specialty Coffee Association of America
1998, 2001 - 2013

STEAK HOUSE & MARKET FRESH FISH

Tampa • Celebration • Orlando

4444 West Cypress Street • Tampa, Florida 33607
Telephone 813-353-9706 • FAX 813-353-9510

Lakeland

St. Petersburg

Orlando

Lake Buena Vista

Orlando

Orlando
Lake Mary

RED LOBSTER...THE BEGINNING

Appetizers

House Cold-Smoked Atlantic Salmon — 8.95
Fresh Salmon Lightly Smoked Over Citrus and Oak Wood, Served Classically with Cream Cheese, Capers, Eggs and Red Onion

Seared Rare Tuna Sashimi — 13.50
Served with a Citrus Sesame, Ginger and Wasabi

Florida Stone Crabs (In Season) — MKT

Charley's Steak Tar Tar — 14.95
Hand Selected Cuts of Tenderloin Finely Chopped, Seasoned and Ready to Mix Tableside. Also Tuna Tar Tar When Available.

Jumbo Shrimp Cocktail — 12.95
Served Icy Cold with a Delightful Homemade Cocktail Sauce

Crispy Portobello Mushroom Fondue — 9.95
Truffled Portobello "Fries" With Applewood Smoked Bacon, Scallions And Crispy Mixed Herbs.

Lobster Bisque — 8.95
Rich and Creamy Bisque Bursting with Maine lobster Served with North Atlantic Swordfish Croutons

Beefsteak Tomato & Vidalia Onion Vinaigrette — 6.95
With Crumbled Maytag Bleu Cheese

Shrimp and Scallop Scampi — 13.95
Large Gulf Shrimp and Scallops Baked in Pure Butter, Garlic, Fresh Parsley, Cognac and Parmesan Herb Bread Crumbs

Escargot Bourgogne — 8.95
Baked in Garlic Butter and Served with Herb and Garlic Toast

Florida Gator — 7.95
A Unique Florida Taste Treat

Charley's Hand Breaded Shrimp — 11.95
Five Fresh Hand Breaded Shrimp Fried Golden Brown and Served with Vidalia Dill Tartar Sauce

Beef Tenderloin Carpaccio — 15.95
Our Best Selected Tenderloin Cuts Seasoned & Seared, Chilled, Then Sliced Thinly. Served with Capers, Red Onions & Alioli Sauce.

Pan Fried Calamari — 10.95
With Fried Red, Green and Yellow Peppers, Garlic and Scallions

Shrimp La Bella — 14.95
A Delicious Portabella Mushroom Cap Stuffed with Charley's Rockefeller Mix, 3 Jumbo Shrimp Covered with Provolone Cheese and Hollandaise Sauce

Market Fresh Fish

Oak Grilled - Blackened - Bronzed
(Some Selections Available In Season Only)

Tuna

Swordfish

Salmon

Mahi-Mahi

Pompano

Cobia

Wahoo

Mako Shark

Gulf Tuna

Rainbow Trout

Red Snapper

Yellow Tail

Gulf Black Grouper

Sauces, Salsa and Butters - 3.00

Cajun Bronzed Sauce

Dill Cream Sauce

Roasted Tomato Vinaigrette

Charley's Marsala Sauce

Pineapple Mango Salsa

Au Poivre Peppercorn Sauce

Szechuan Vinaigrette

Hollandaise / Béarnaise

From the Deep Blue Sea

All entrées served with Charley's signature house salad, garlic cheese butter bread and creamery fresh butter.

Alaskan King Crab — 1 lb - MKT   1½ lb - MKT
Succulent Red King Crab Served Steamed with a Side of Drawn Butter.

Florida Stone Crab, (2-1/4 lbs.) — In Season
(In Season Only) Chilled Crabs Cracked and Served with Mustard Sauce. Just like "Joe's Made Them Famous".

Jumbo Fried Shrimp — 18.95
Our Extra Jumbo Shrimp Hand Breaded To Order Only. Made Fresh When Each Ticket Enters The Kitchen.

Australian Rock Lobster Tail — 2.75 per ounce
(Ask Your Server For Sizes Available) Tender Lobster Tail Delicately Prepared with Seasoned Bread Crumbs and Fresh Lemon Drawn Butter, Then Baked to Perfection. (Sizes Vary Daily with Availability.)

Mixed Grill — 26.95
Two Select Fish of the Day (Chef's Choice) Served with Our Shrimp and Scallop Scampi.

There is a risk with consuming raw or uncooked proteins. If you have chronic illness of the stomach, liver, blood or have immune disorders you are at a greater risk of serious illness from consuming raw or undercooked proteins.

Gift Cards Available • 20% on Parties of 8 or More

Western Steaks Aged to Perfection

All entrées served with Charley's signature house salad, garlic cheese butter bread and creamery fresh butter.

Charley's Ultimate Surf and Turf (For Two) — 119.95
50 oz. Porterhouse and 1-1/4 lb. Lobster Tail.

Fabulous Filet Mignon (20 oz.) — 64.95
This is a true center cut Filet Mignon, we only get one per loin and two per steer, the most tender cut of all our filets.

Filet Mignon — 8oz - 34.95   12oz - 42.95
The Filet Mignon is the tenderest of all cuts. (Stuffed with Blue Cheese, Add 2.50)

Porterhouse (32 oz.) — 43.95
The Porterhouse is a rich flavorful well aged steak best suited for the hearty appetite.

T-Bone (18 oz.) — 28.95
The T-Bone has the same rich flavor as the Porterhouse, but with a smaller filet. Served bone-in to retain the natural juices.

Kansas City Strip (Bone In) (22 oz.) — 32.95
The Sirloin known for its richness, coupled with our hand-turned aging process and open pit cooking produces the juiciest of steaks! (When available)

New York Strip (18 oz.) — 29.95
A flavorful and tender steak made more tender with our aging process. We serve the New York Strip boneless and well-trimmed. (Topped with au poivre peppercorn sauce add 3.00)

Orange and Oak Grilled to Perfection

Pork Chops (1-1/2" Thick) — Single Chop - 17.95   Double Chops - 21.95
We take the same pride in our Pork Chops as in our steaks, serving you only chops, which have never been frozen, seasoned with fresh herbs and lemon juice, grilled over our natural wood-burning pit to a juicy and tender perfection.

Veal Marsala — 23.95
Gently sautéed bone-in veal chop complimented with our own "Charley's" marsala sauce.

Porterhouse Veal Chop (24 oz.) — 27.95
Milk fed, "double thick" Veal Porterhouse, citrus and oak grilled, basted with lemon parsley butter.

Lamb T-Bone Chops — 26.95
Whole T-Bone Rack of Lamb cooked on our special pit, sliced tableside and served with fresh mint sauce.

Flame-Broiled Chicken Breast — 16.95
Twin tender breast of chicken, marinated in sweet butter and fresh lemon, then grilled on our open pit, the way the Indians used to cook.

Aged to Perfection and Cooked to Your Specifications!

HOW TO ORDER OUR STEAKS TO YOUR TASTE.

Aged meat is already tender by natural process and aged meat is never bloody. Therefore, you can order your steak done to a lesser degree than you would if you were eating fresh meat. In fact, aged meat becomes tougher the longer you cook it, while fresh meat is cooked longer to tenderize it. Order your steak exactly the way you'd like it broiled. If you'd like a thicker steak (like the Filet Mignon) broiled medium well or well done, it will be "butterflied" to insure it is evenly cooked and the flavor is retained.

RARE . . . Brown-Seared Crust with a Cool Red Center

MEDIUM RARE . . . Brown-Seared Crust with a Warm Red Center

MEDIUM . . . Outside of Steak Well Done, Dark Brown with a Hot Pink Center

MEDIUM WELL . . . Outside Dark Brown, Inside Done with a Thin Line of Pink in the Center, But Still Juicy

WELL . . . Outside Dark Brown, Center Cooked Thoroughly

**PLEASE ALLOW ADDITIONAL TIME FOR STEAKS COOKED MEDIUM WELL OR WELL
TOTALLY RESPONSIBLE FOR STEAKS COOKED WELL DONE (IF BUTTERFLIED)**

Side Orders

Sautéed Mushrooms & Onions — 6.95	Garlic Bread — 2.75	Jumbo Fresh Asparagus or Fresh Vegetables — 6.95
Fresh Oak-Grilled Vegetables — 5.95	Shrimp Scallop Scampi — 13.95	Creamed Spinach — 6.95
10 oz. Australian Rock Lobster Tail with any steak entrée — 27.50	Bleu Cheese Crumbles or Steakhouse Bacon Lardons *Delicious on salad, potato or steak* — 2.50	Fried Green Tomatoes — 5.95
		Charley's Smashed, Baked or Au Gratin Potato — 4.00

Please - No Separate Checks on Parties of Eight or More

VITO'S CHOP HOUSE
International Drive
Established 1998

AGED STEAKS ♦ FINE WINES ♦ PREMIUM CIGARS

At Vito's Chop House, we remember the pleasure of dining the old-fashioned way, the way of Vito, Tony, and Gino Carlucci, who arrived in New York over 50 years ago from Florence, Italy. Full of pride, dreams, and ideas, the three brothers' first job in America was in Little Italy, where they worked as cooks and learned to speak English.

After years of long hours and hard work, Gino and Tony opened their restaurant in Brooklyn, New York. Meanwhile, Vito had gone to work in the stockyards as a butcher. Vito cut the steaks for some of the famous steakhouses in New York, like Peter Luger's, Palm, Sparks and Gallagher's. Here he learned the secrets of what to look for to create the best Steaks. The secrets were the type of animals, the size and age of the animals, whose farm it came from, and the time and temperature of the aging. These secrets, along with the love of the restaurant business, have been passed down to a new generation of Carlucci's, whose goal and commitment is to create an environment reminiscent of the fine dining style our father and uncles enjoyed providing to their guests.

Our focus is on a total quality dining experience, in the food we offer, it's preparation and in the service we provide...quality knows no shortcuts.

We serve only the finest USDA Prime and Choice Beef aged in our meat lockers 4-6 weeks. We cook our steaks, chops, the Tuscan way, very hot and fast, over orange, oak and mystique wood fire.

Fresh Fish? Our personal Fishmonger goes to the boats and hand-picks each individual fish. The only way to tell he is fresh is to look him square in his eye: the eyes should be clear, gills bright red, the smell should be like a fresh cut cucumber. No fish odor!

We offer an extensive cellar with over 1400 wines to complement your meal. Our wine steward and knowledgeable staff will be happy to assist you in your selection.

Treat yourself to a delectable homemade dessert, or enjoy a fine cigar along with a glass of aged cognac, armagnac or grappa in our lounge.

At Vito's we strive to give excellent service at all times. If by chance we displease you in any way, please ask for Terry, Adam, Christian or John immediately!

Thank You very much for dining here. *Vito*

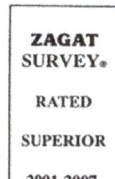

RED LOBSTER...THE BEGINNING

Appetizers

Mussels Marinière 9
Fresh PEI mussels simmered in a fragrant broth of white wine, celery and tomatoes.

Beef Carpaccio* 13
Seasoned, seared-tenderloin thinly sliced and drizzled with a unique Creole aioli. Topped with fresh Reggiano-parmesan and mixed arugula greens.

Colossal U-10 Shrimp .... (5) 11
.... famous large platter (12) 20
Served icy cold with our homemade cocktail sauce and sweet pepper rouille.

Crispy Eggplant Fries 9
Semolina-parmesan crusted with roasted red pepper aioli & crispy herbs.

Lobster Bisque 12
Rich and creamy bisque bursting with Maine lobster and served with North Atlantic swordfish croutons.

Shrimp Scampi Croustade 12
Fresh baked parmesan focaccia with jumbo white prawns in a white wine lemon basil beurre blanc.

Crab Cake alla Milanese 15
Romano crusted jumbo lump crab with roasted peppers and fresh arugula.

Mozzarella Malazon 8
Imported mozzarella cheese fried then topped with marinara sauce and provolone cheese.

Pan Fried Calamari .... small platter 8
.... large platter 13
Sautéed with an assortment of red, yellow and green, banana, cherry and bell peppers.

Tuna Tar Tare* (for 2) 16
Sundried tomato marinade, capers and asiago cheese served with parmesan crostini and roasted red pepper rouille.

Seasonal Oysters

Baked Rockefeller	Crab Stuffed	Crispy Pancetta	Shucked Oysters
Creamy spinach topped with provolone and hollandaise.	Lump crab and roasted red pepper aioli.	Parmesan aioli and crispy pancetta.	1/2 dozen ... 11 Full dozen ... 18
11	12	11	Fresh from Florida.

Oyster Trio 12
2 of each specialty baked oyster

• • • Antipasto Platters • • •

The Venetian	The Campania	The Tuscany
Pan-fried calamari, tuna tar tare with parmesan crostini and char-grilled octopus with tomato vinaigrette.	Thyme roasted portabella with basil tomato vinaigrette and almond encrusted goat cheese in a sundried tomato pesto.	Reggiano-parmesan, mortadella, tartufo formaggio, imported gorgonzola and proscuitto with cipollini agrodolce.
15	14	15

Salads

Vito's Wedge	Heirloom Tomatoes & Bufala Mozzarella	The Caesar
Baby iceberg, tomato, gorgonzola, and crispy mortadella with homemade ranch.	Fresh basil, pesto, balsamic vinegar and extra virgin olive oil.	Crisp romaine, pancetta, baby croutons and fresh grated Reggiano-Parmesan. with anchovies....... add .50
5	7	6

Pasta

Vito's Meatballs Pomodoro 16
Vito's house made meatballs simmered in our marinara sauce and served over rigatoni or linguine.

Shrimp and Scallop Scampi 29
Jumbo Gulf shrimp and sea scallops sautéed with fresh garlic, extra virgin olive oil and fresh herbs. Served over a bed of linguine.

Rigatoni Rustica 19
Italian sausage, roasted sweet peppers, broccoli rapini and Roma tomatoes.

Truffled Lobster Ravioli 35
Sweet lobster ravioli with seasonal fresh Maine lobster and white truffle sherry cream.

Penne alla Vodka 23
Creamy San Marzano tomato sauce, proscuitto and parmesan.

Butternut Squash Ravioli 18
Finished with a fresh sage and brown butter sauce with grated reggiano-parmesan.

*Consumer Information: Consuming raw or undercooked meats, poultry, seafood or eggs may increase your risk of foodborne illness, especially if you have certain medical conditions. There is a risk associated with consuming raw oysters. If you have chronic illness of the liver, stomach or blood, or have immune disorders, you are at greater risk of serious illness from raw oysters, and should eat oysters fully cooked. If unsure of your risk, consult a physician.

RESTAURANTS

Prime Seafood and Fresh Fish

Cedar Plank Roasted King Salmon 29
King Salmon topped with Parmesan-red onion aioli and placed on a cedar plank for roasting over our custom citrus and oak wood-burning pit.

Gulf Flounder Picatta *Fresh Florida* 28
Pan seared local flounder with lemon, capers and white wine. Served with broccoli rabe.

Mediterranean Barbeque Tuna Mignon 34
Peppercorn crusted "Ahi" tuna mignon, seared rare and served with crispy herbs and our signature sauce.

Swordfish au Poivre 31
Fresh swordfish, lightly encrusted with sliced almonds and spice, finished with our au poivre peppercorn sauce. Accompanied by potatoes rapini.

Vito's Seasonal Features

Veal Brunello (when available) 36
Mozzarella and herbs stuffed Provini veal chop pan sautéed with sun-dried tomato and goat cheese.

Lobster Cioppino 38
A traditional seafood dish of fresh Maine lobster, Gulf shrimp, sea scallops and chunks of white fish cooked in a light saffron, tomato and white wine broth.

Chicken Fricassée 19
Classic Italian style sautéed herb encrusted chicken with pan roasted vegetables and smashed potatoes.

Tuscan Style Steaks and Chops

T-Bone 20 oz 36	Filet Mignon, 8 oz 37
Porterhouse 25 oz 40	Filet Mignon, 12 oz 42
Porterhouse Veal Chop 2½" thick 35	Prime Ribeye, 24 oz Bone-in 39

Pork Chops di Vito 2" thick 23
topped with assorted peppers & piccata sauce

Steaks for Two

Tomahawk Long Bone Ribeye 99	**Vito's Master Cut** 75
30 ounce Greg Norman Wagyu "Kobe" Ribeye, carved tableside and served with roasted garlic and fresh herbs.	52 ounce porterhouse cut 2 1/2" thick. Citrus grilled and served with Piemontese butter.

Rare - cool red center • **Medium Rare** - warm red center • **Medium** - hot pink center
Medium Well - thin line of pink • **Well** - cooked thoroughly

Finishing Touches...

Truffled Horseradish Aioli . . . 2

Au Poivre Cognac Peppercorn Sauce . . . 2.50

Béarnaise or Hollandaise . . . 2

Gorgonzola Crumbles . . . 3.50

Make Your Entree Surf...

Crab Stuffed Shrimp . . . 7.50
Lump crab and red pepper aioli

Oscar Style . . . 6.50
Crab, asparagus and hollandaise

Stuffed Lobster Tail . . . 12
Stuffed with Cape May scallop gratinese

Potatoes, Vegetables and Sides

Sautéed Mushrooms 2.75	Creamy Spinach 4	Scallion Smashed Potatoes 4
Firenze Fries 4.50	Oak-Grilled Vegetables 5	Potatoes Rapini 5.50
Pan Roasted Vegetables 6	Sautéed Broccoli 4	
Giant Baked Potato ATW 4	Fried Green Tomatoes 4.50	Fresh Jumbo Asparagus........6 with hollandaise

Gift Cards Available • 17% Gratuity on Parties of 6 or More • Private Function Dining Rooms

RED LOBSTER...THE BEGINNING

MOONFISH
Sand Lake Road
Established 2002

MOONFISH

RESTAURANTS

2011 America's Top Ten
SEAFOOD HOUSES

Tom Horan's America's Top Ten Club is proud to name our list of America's Top Ten Seafood Houses* for 2011:

1. **MoonFish**
   ORLANDO, FLORIDA
2. **Elliott's Oyster House**
   SEATTLE, WASHINGTON
3. **Bourbon House**
   NEW ORLEANS, LOUISIANA
4. **Emeril's New Orleans Fish House**
   LAS VEGAS, NEVADA
5. **Anthony's Pier 4**
   BOSTON, MASSACHUSETTS
6. **Cafe Pacific**
   DALLAS, TEXAS
7. **Union Oyster House**
   BOSTON, MASSACHUSETTS
8. **Osetra**
   SAN DIEGO, CALIFORNIA
9. **Tony Mandola's Gulf Coast Kitchen**
   HOUSTON, TEXAS
10. **Oceana**
    NEW YORK, NEW YORK

*Independent Establishments
WWW.TOMHORAN.COM

RED LOBSTER...THE BEGINNING

Fresh Shellfish Bar

Baked Oysters Rockerfeller	Coast to Coast Oyster Array	Wood Roasted Oysters
11.95	12.95	12.95

○ Iced Shellfish Tower...29.95
Fresh Gulf Oysters, Jumbo Shrimp, Alaskan King Crab and Steamed Mussels

Appetizers

MoonFish Steak Tar-Tar...15.95
Traditional or Pan-Asian

Crackling Five Spice Calamari Kung Pao	10.95
Toasted Coconut Shrimp	9.95
Crab Louis Wonton	16.95
○ Sesame Duck Carpaccio	7.25
○ Seared Rare Tuna Sashimi	
Half order .... 8.50 Full order 15.95	
Shrimp Remoulade	12.95
○ MoonFish Seafood Cocktail	14.95
Pan Asian Ceviche Style with Shrimp, Fish, and Lobster	
Crab Cake	15.95
Crispy Almond fried Lobster Tails	24.95
○ Wok-Fried Soft Shell Crab	12.95
○ Beefsteak Tomato and Buffalo Mozzarella	8.95
○ Alaskan King Crab	13.95
Crab Claws (Seasonal Selection)	MKT
Tuna Tar-Tar Tacos	12.95

Bait Bar Sampler
22.50
···· "Real King Crab" California Roll ···· Spicy Ahi Tuna Tar-Tar ····
···· Shrimp Avocado Super Crunch Roll ····

Mussels

These mussels are farm raised by Ron Jayson of Prince Edward Island. His mussel farm lies along Orwell Cove in pristine waters where the tide rises and falls 12 feet per day, flushing and refreshing the water around his mussels.

Thai Red Curry...12.95
Spicy coconut milk broth with lemongrass, Siamese ginger, pineapple & Thai basil

Marinière...12.95
Garlic, butter, shallots and white wine

17% Gratuity on parties of 6 or more

One check only on parties of 6 or more, $5.00 Share Charge

General Manager	Mary DiMatteo
Service Ambassadors	Brian Fry & Richard Lykins
Cellar Master	Brian Callan
Chef	Kenny James
Special Events Coordinator	Andrea Angst
Corporate Chef	Dan Drayer
Operating Partner	Seth A. Miller

Steaks ○ Chops ○ Etc...

 USDA CHOICE   USDA PRIME

Aged 4-6 Weeks ···· Citrus & Oak Wood Fired ···· Hand Cut Daily

○ "King of the Bone" New York Strip 20oz	28.95
○ Filet Mignon 12-13oz	33.95
Oscar Mignon (Blue Crab, Soft Shell Crab, Asparagus & Hollandaise)	35.95
○ Prime Ribeye 24oz (Bone-in)	31.95
○ Grilled Pork Chops (2" Thick)	16.95
Shanghai Duck Breast (Sesame, Soy, Ginger, Pineapple Marinade)	16.95
○ Hawaiian-Style Double Chicken Breast	14.95

All Steaks Can Surf...
Sea Scallop Skewer	10.95
10oz Green Back Lobster Tail Broiled or Fried	24.95
Alaskan Red King Crab (3/4 pound)	13.95
Jumbo Fried Shrimp	9.95
Shrimp & Scallop Scampi	12.95

Bleu Cheese Stuffed ○ $2.95	Sandeman's 20yr Port Wine Glaze $8.95 w/Gorgonzola Butter	Pan Asian "Oscar" $8.95	Classic Style $7.95	MoonFish Oscar $11.95

The above entrees include Jeannine's Frenchmaid bread, MoonFish house salad and choice of baked potato, scallion mashed potatoes or east-west fries.

Lobster ○ Crab ○ Shrimp

Grilled or Crispy Almond Batter-Fried Green Back Lobster Tail 1 - 1 1/4 lbs	49.95
($2.75 per ounce over 1 1/4 lbs) Ask your server for available sizes.	
Twin Caribbean Thai Style Lobster Tail with Thai Basil	49.95
○ Bamboo Steamer	31.95
Lobster Tail, King Crab, Fish, Shrimp & Steamed Fresh Vegetables	
○ MoonFish Bouillabaisse	29.95
Lobster, King Crab, Shrimp & Fish	
○ Alaskan Red King Crab 1 1/4 lbs	29.95
○ Florida Stone Crab 2 1/4 lbs (In Season Only)	MKT
Served cold with Johnnie's famous mustard sauce	
Shrimp & Scallop Scampi	19.95
Jumbo Lump Crabmeat Stuffed Shrimp & Scallops	25.95
Jumbo Hand Breaded Shrimp (6) 16.95 (8)	21.95
All You Can Eat (Absolutely No Sharing!!!)	29.95

Above entrees include Jeannine's Frenchmaid bread, MoonFish house salad, steamed ginger vegetables and sticky rice.

Prime Seafood
Our Seafood is under the HACCP Government Inspection Program and is based on Daily availability only!

Sides to Share

Sautéed mushrooms and onions	3.95		
Creamed spinach	4.50	Lobster gravy mashed potatoes	5.95
○ Oak-grilled asparagus	5.95	Bleu cheese mashed potatoes	5.50
Fried green tomatoes	3.95	Scallion mashed potatoes	2.95
East-west fries	2.75	Giant baked potato	2.75
Szechuan green beans	3.95	Wok-steamed ginger veggies	3.95

The Freshest Seafood from the Oceans of Planet Earth!

Consumer Information: There is a risk associated with consuming raw oysters. If you have chronic illness of the liver, stomach, or blood, or have immune disorders, you are at a greater risk of serious illness from raw oysters and should eat oysters fully cooked. If unsure of your risk, consult a physician.

MoonFish ○ 7525 West Sand Lake Road ○ Orlando, Florida ○ 32819 ○ 407.363.7262 ○ 407.345.0097 fax

○ Denotes Chef's Healthy Choice Selections

RESTAURANTS

Friday, July 11, 2014

Chef Marcus' Seasonal Specialties

Filet and Lobster center cut filet paired scallop crusted Maine lobster tail..................43.95
Wagyu Tomahawk Ribeye a long bone ribeye with garlic mash potatoes....................99.95
Beef Short Rib Ravioli served in a creamy port glaze 24.95

Shokunin

Ahi Tuna Pizza..16.95
Izuma Dai 14.95
Hawaiian Roll 16.95

Japanese Pizza

Fresh Salmon	Yellowtail
Basil Pesto, Snow Crab, Red Onion, And Lemon Zest	Fresh Jalapeno and Micro-Cilantro with Eel sauce, Jalapeno Aioli, and White Truffle Oil
$15.95	$16.95

Fresh Fish Today

Macadamia Crusted Pacific Mahi-Mahi served with mango pineapple salsa and sticky rice..........32.95
Caught by Jimmy Harris off the coast of Guatemala

Jumbo Lump Crab Crusted Chilean Sea Bass with mirin-wasabi glaze and sticky rice............38.95
Caught by Captain Skinner off the coast of Tierra del Fuego **"Featured at the James Beard House"**

Blackened Pacific Swordfish with lobster gravy mashed potatoes.......................................26.95
Caught by Captain J. McGlashen off coast of Ecuador

Lobster Encrusted Hawaiian Trigger Fish with Lobster Sherry Cream........................ 34.95
Caught by Richard Narcisi off the coast of the Big Island

Crispy Whole Yellow Tail Snapper with kung pao sauce and Japanese sticky rice 33.95
Caught by: Bobby Johnson off the coast of Nicaragua

Hong Kong Halibut with sautéed spinach and sticky rice in a light sherry soy 35.95
Caught in Winter Harbor off the coast of Alaska

Cedar Plank Atlantic King Salmon with red onion and Parmesan aioli and 29.95
Line-caught off the Coast of New England by Captain Kevin McCullen

Gulf Black Grouper topped with mushrooms, king crab and citrus buerre blanc..............................33.95
Caught by: Andrew Massa in the Gulf of Mexico

Nori Crusted Yellow-Fin "Ahi" Tuna with cilantro salad and sweet Thai chili buerre blanc 36.95
Caught by: Captain H. Kalahani Loran off the coast of Venezuela

Stuffed Australian Barramundi jumbo lump crab, shrimp and brie with Szechwan green beans...........27.95
Caught in the watersheds of the Victoria River in Northern Australia.

Rainbow Trout Meunière in brown butter, shitake mushrooms, and lemon with Szechwan green beans 18.95
Farm Raised in Colombia

Whole Yellow Tail Snapper on a 1500 degree Citrus and Oak pit with fire roasted cream corn 32.95
Caught by: Bobby Johnson off the coast of Nicaragua

Above entrées served with seasonal house salad and homemade buttery cheese bread

RED LOBSTER...THE BEGINNING

FISHBONES
Lake Mary
Established 2005

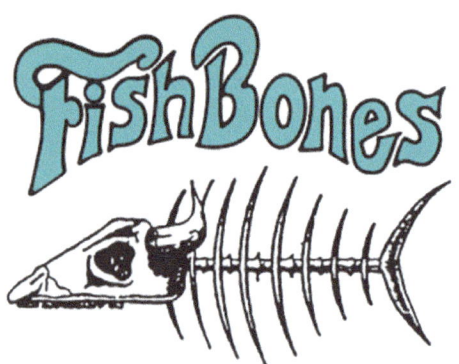

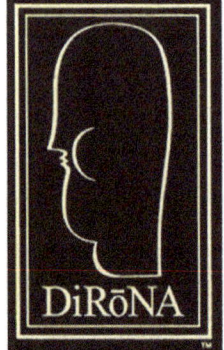

~~Fresh Shellfish Bar~~

Coast to Coast Oyster Array 13.95
2 oysters from each region

Prime Salty Seas, Florida	....	each 1.95
Bon Secour, Texas	....	each 1.95
Fanny Bays, British Columbia	....	each 2.95
Malpeques, Canada	....	each 2.95

Yuzu Lemon Vinaigrette	Classic Cocktail Sauce	Asian Ponzu Sauce

Oysters Rockefeller 6 Prime Salty Seas Oysters 12.95	Crab Stuffed Oysters 6 Prime Salty Seas Oysters 13.95

King Crab Legs 3/4 lbs. 14.95
Served Cold or Hot

Jumbo Lump Blue Crab Martini 11.95

Seasonal Crab Claws .... MKT
Served Cold with Johnnies Famous Mustard Sauce

Jumbo Shrimp Cocktail 12.95

Jumbo Shrimp Remoulade 12.95

Smokey BBQ Shrimp 1/2 lbs. 10.95
(u-peel-um) Messy, but Worth It. (Served chilled)

> **Raw Bar Platter** 37.95
> Jumbo Shrimp Cocktail, Oysters on the Half Shell, Jumbo Lump Crab Cocktail, Chilled Steamed Mussels, 1/4 lb. Smokey BBQ Shrimp & Shrimp Remoulade.

~~Appetizers~~

Fried Calamari 8.95
Sautéed Red, Yellow, Green, Banana & Cherry Peppers. Tossed with Flash Fried Calamari. Served with Marinara Sauce.

Blue Chips 7.95
Homemade Blue Cheese Crema Topped Potato Chips. "You Can't Eat Just One."

Bahamian Smoked Fish Dip 5.95
Buttonwood Smoked Fresh Fish.

Escargot 8.95
Baked in Fresh Butter, Garlic, Cognac & Parsley. Served with Garlic Bread.

New England Clam Chowder ..... cup 3.25 / bowl 4.50

Florida Gator 7.95
"Tastes Like Chicken" Maybe It Ate One.

Cold Smoked Scottish Salmon 8.95
House Smoked with Citrus & Alder Wood.

Wild Blue Mussels 1 & 1/4 lbs. 8.95
Pan-roasted with White Wine, Garlic, Tomatoes & Butter.

Seared-Rare Tuna Sashimi ...... half order 8.95 / full order 15.50

Crispy Almond Fried Lobster Tail 26.95
Served with Orange Blossom Honey.

> **Bait Bar Sampler**
> **22.50**
> -- "Real Canadian Crab" California Roll --
> -- Yum-Yum Roll -- Tuna Toro Nachos --

Chef Dan's ~~Seasonal Features~~

> **Lobster "Cappuccino"** 8.95
> Creamy Lobster Bisque with Blue Lump Crab topped with Sherry Cream
>
> **Jumbo Lump Crab Cake Appetizer** 15.95
> Served with a Pineapple Mango Salsa
>
> **Toshi's "Trio" Sushi Special** 22.95
> Double Spicy Tuna, Shrimp Tempura, and Spider Roll
>
> **FishBones Sushi Tour** 29.95
> Rainbow Roll, Chef Choice 6 pc. Sashimi & Free Tuna Toro Nachos

North American Bison Ribeye 40.95
Served with a Warm Gorgonzola Fondue

Macadamia Crusted Mahi 31.95
Paired with a Pineapple Mango Salsa and Coconut Mango Sauce

Jumbo Lump Crab Cake Entree 29.95
With a Pineapple Mango Salsa

Szechuan Ahi Tuna Mignon (served rare) ... 33.95
Pan Seared with a Toasted Sesame Seed-Peppercorn Crust

FishBones Oscar Mignon 39.95
Topped with Jumbo Lump Crab, Soft Shell Crab, Asparagus, Hollandaise Sauce

Seafood Trio 34.95
Chef's Choice of Oak Grilled Fish with Crab Stuffed Shrimp and Scallops

Mirin Wasabi Glazed Sea Bass 45.95
With a Lump Blue Crab Crust, Cool Crab Salad & Mirin-Lemon Butter Sauce

Crispy Snapper Meuniere Style 31.95
Whole fried Florida Lane snapper served with capers, shitake mushrooms in a brown butter sauce. Caught in the Florida Keys.

Fresh Fish Today

Blackened — Broiled — Citrus & Oak Grilled

Meuniere	Mushroom Crab Beurre Blanc	Oscar Style	Classic Style
4.95	8.95	8.95	8.95

Yellowfin "Ahi" Tuna .... MKT
Landed off Fort Pierce

Mahi Mahi .... MKT
Caught off the Costa Rican Coast

Black Grouper .... MKT
Caught off Sombrero Key

Chilean Sea Bass .... MKT
Caught off the Southern Pointe of Chile

Atlantic Salmon .... MKT
Caught off the coast of Newfoundland

> **Whole Fish** --- Florida Lane Snapper
>
> Herb Marinated and Oak Grilled
> Cooked Whole over Citrus & Oak Wood.   28.95

Planked Fish

Atlantic Salmon
26.95
Topped with a Parmesan-Red Onion Aioli
Served with Mashed Potatoes & Wok Steamed Ginger Vegetables

RED LOBSTER...THE BEGINNING

Shell Fish

Jumbo Fried Shrimp......................(8 Shrimp) ...18.95
Our Extra Jumbo Shrimp are Hand Breaded to Order Only!
Made Fresh When Each Ticket Enters the Kitchen.

All-U-Can-Eat Jumbo Fried Shrimp......................24.95
Same as Above Except You Decide When to Say Enough is Enough

Stuffed Shrimp & Scallops......................26.95
A Combination of Jumbo Gulf Shrimp and Sea Scallops, topped with Lump Crab
Meat and a White Wine Butter Sauce.

Shrimp & Scallop Scampi......................21.95
Large Gulf Shrimp & Jumbo Canadian Sea Scallops Baked in Pure Butter,
Garlic, Fresh Parsley, Cognac & topped with Parmesan Herb Bread Crumbs.

King Crab (1 1/2 lbs.)......................29.95
Succulent Alaskan Red King Crab served Steamed with
a side of Drawn Butter.

Florida Stone Crab (2 1/4 lbs.)......................MKT
(In season only) Chilled Crabs Cracked & Served with Mustard Sauce.
Just like "Joe's Made Them Famous".

Australian Rock Lobster Tail (1-1 1/4 lbs.)......................49.95
(2.00 per oz. Over 1 1/4 lbs.) Tender Lobster Tail Delicately Prepared
with Seasoned Breadcrumbs, Fresh Lemon, Drawn Butter & then
baked to Perfection.

FishBones Bouillabaisse......................27.95
Lobster, King Crab, Gulf Shrimp & Fresh Fish
In a Saffron Broth with White Rice

*Served with Jeannine's Frenchmaid Bread, FishBones Signature Salad,
Wok Steamed Ginger Vegetables & Tropical Saffron Orzo.*

Live Maine Lobsters

1.5 lb. Lobster

Ask Server for Today's Available Sizes...MKT
(per oz. Over 2 lbs.)

39.95
• **Steamed** served with lemon & drawn butter.
• **Citrus & Oak Wood Grilled**
• **Broiled** topped with seasoned bread crumbs & drawn butter.

Baked Lobster & Crab Stuffed......................45.95
Stuffed with FishBones Famous Crab Stuffing, Topped with
Seasoned Bread Crumbs then Baked until Hot & Golden Brown.

Salads

Classic Wedge......................5.95
Crisp Iceberg Lettuce Served with Buttermilk Blue Cheese Dressing,
Crumbled Blue Cheese, Chopped Tomato & Crisp Bacon.

Beefsteak Tomato & Bufala Mozzarella......................10.95
Red & Yellow Tomatoes, Fresh Basil, Bufala Mozzarella,
Basil Pesto & Kalamata Olives.

Dried Cherry & Goat Cheese Salad......................6.95
Organic Spring Mix, Crumbled Laura Chenel Goat Cheese,
Sun Dried Cherries, Toasted Pine Nuts with Citrus Soy Vinaigrette.

Julius Caesar......................5.95
Crisp Romaine Lettuce, Freshly Shaved Reggiano Parmesan Cheese,
Toasted Garlic Croutons. (anchovies optional)

Bones

20/20 Surf & Turf......................99.95
"The Ultimate Surf & Turf" Either for One or for Two.
20 oz. Center Cut Filet Mignon/20 oz. Lobster Tail.

Filet Mignon 12-13 oz.......................33.95
The Tenderest of all Steak Cuts. We Select & Buy the Heaviest
USDA Prime & Choice Western Grain-fed Tenderloins & Properly
Age Them for that Tender, Flavorful & Sweet Taste.
Stuffed with fresh blue cheese crumbles. Add 2.50

"King of the Bone" New York Strip 20-22 oz...31.95
Thick USDA Choice Strip Aged Six Weeks on Premise,
Trimmed within 1/8" for Maximum Flavor.
Topped with Bearnaise. Add 2.50

Kabob (when available)......................16.95
Choice Chunks of Filet Mignon & New York Strip. Served with Onions,
Peppers & Tomatoes, Skewered & Grilled to Perfection. (while they last)

Dry Aged Ribeye......................42.95
28oz Long Bone-Ribeye Old School Dry Aging Method
for 21 Days makes this Steak Beefy Rich & Extremely Flavorful.
Tender as a Mother's Love.

All Steaks Can Surf...
• Port Wine Glaze......................5.95
  with Gorgonzola Butter.
• Oscar Style......................8.95
• Maytag Blue Cheese Stuffed......................2.50
• 10 oz. Green Back Lobster Tail......................25.95
• Mushroom & Crab Beurre Blanc......................8.95
• Alaskan Red King Crab 3/4lb......................14.95
• Jumbo Blackened Shrimp......................9.50

*Served with Jeannine's Homemade Bread, FishBones Signature Salad
& Sea Salt Encrusted Baked Potato or Rosemary Parmesan Garlic Fries.*

1200°F

How to order our steaks to your taste:

RARE-Brown-Seared crust with cool red center.

MEDIUM RARE-Brown-Seared crust with a warm red center.

MEDIUM-Outside of steak well done, dark brown crust with hot pink center.

MEDIUM WELL-Outside dark brown, inside done with a thin line of pink in the center but still juicy.

WELL-Outside dark brown, center cooked thoroughly.

Aged to Perfection and Cooked to Your Specifications!

Prime Rib

Our Prime Rib is Slow Roasted for 23 Hours in Our Specially-built Oven using
Oak & Citrus Wood. This Cooking Procedure will Provide the Most Tender,
Juicy Prime Rib Possible. Served with Au Jus & Horseradish Sauce.
Roasted Fresh Daily While They Last. Sorry Only Two End Cuts per Roast!

Prime Rib of Beef - 16 oz.......................28.95

Hearty Cut - 24 oz. (Bone In)......................31.95

—**Blackened & Plank Roasted 3.95**—

*Served with Jeannine's Homemade Bread, FishBones Signature Salad
& Sea Salt Encrusted Baked Potato or Rosemary Parmesan Garlic Fries.*

Prime Seafood
Our Seafood is under the HACCP Government Inspection Program
and is based on Daily Availability Only!

🐟 Denotes Chef's Healthy Choice Selections.

*Consumer Information: There is a risk associated with consuming raw oysters.
If you have chronic illness of the liver, stomach, or blood, or
have immune disorders, You are at a greater risk of serious illness
from raw oysters and should eat oysters fully cooked.
If unsure of your risk, consult a physician.*

RESTAURANTS

Sushi Chef
~~~ Seasonal Creations ~~~

Tuna Won Ton Tacos 11.95
With Edamane Dip & Seaweed Salad.

Ahi Tuna Trio 15.95
Hawaiian Poke, Cajun Blackened & Japanese Tataki.

Traditional Bait

		Sushi 2 Pc. with Rice	Sashimi 3 Pc. with out Rice
1.	Tuna (Maguro)	8.00	10.50
2.	Yellowtail (Hamachi)	8.00	10.50
3.	White Meat Fish	4.25	5.00
4.	Fresh Salmon (Sake)	7.00	9.50
5.	Shrimp (Ebi)	4.00	- . - -
6.	Crab (Kani)	4.00	6.25
7.	Octopus (Tako)	4.50	5.50
8.	Squid (Ika)	4.00	5.50
9.	Eel (Unagi)	5.00	7.50
10.	Smoked Salmon (Sake Kunsei)	4.50	5.50
11.	Conch (Horagai)	4.50	5.00
12.	Scallops (Hotate)	4.50	6.50 (2pc)
13.	Sweet Shrimp w/ heads (Amaebi)	5.95	5.25 (2pc)
14.	Sea Urchin (Uni)	5.25 (1pc)	8.00 (2pc)
15.	Mackerel (Shime Saba)	4.50	5.50
16.	Escolar (White Tuna)	4.95	5.25
17.	Tuna Belly		10.00 (2pc)
18.	Salmon Roe (Ikura)	5.50	6.50

~~~~~~~ Tobikos & Caviars ~~~~~~~

Wasabi Tobiko	4.95	Jalapeno Tobiko	4.95
Black Tobiko	4.95	Yuzu Tobiko	4.95
Special Red Tobiko	4.95		

(2 pieces per order)

Tobiko Array *Choice of all 5 flavors* 11.95

New Style Bait

19. **Tuna Toro Nachos** *with Nori Chips & Jalapeno Flying Fish Roe.* 15.95
20. **Hamachi Tiradito** *with Yuzu Lemon, Sriracha & Cilantro.* 13.95
21. **Escolar & Avocado Sashimi** *with Citrus Ponzu.* 11.95

~~~~~~~ Signature Oysters ~~~~~~~

23. **Oyster Shooter** *Served with Sake, Ponzu and chopped shiso leaf with Quail egg and Tobiko* 7.95
24. **Sashimi Oysters** *(2pc) with Yuzu, Lemon & Daikon Sprouts.* 4.95
25. **Pan-Asian Oysters** *Baked with Cilantro Pesto.* 4.95
26. **Oyster Japanaise** *(2pc) Oysters served with Ponzu Sauce & Seaweed.* 5.50

Classic Rolls

California Roll 9.00
"Real Crab Meat" Rolled with Avocado, Masago & Cucumber.

Spicy Double Tuna 16.50
Spicy Marinated Tuna Wrapped in Nori .Topped with Sliced Tuna, Scallions & Red Pepper Aioli.

Shrimp Tempura 8.50
Crispy Fried Shrimp with Avocado, Cream Cheese, Masago Aioli & Eel Sauce drizzle.

Dynamite 10.95
Tuna & Yellowtail Roll with Japanese Mayonnaise & Fresh Wasabi.

Rainbow 11.95
"Real Canadian Crab" Roll Topped with Shrimp, White Fish, Tuna, Yellowtail, Fresh Salmon & Avocado.

Volcano 15.95
"Canadian Crab" Rolled with Avocado & Cucumber. Topped with a Spicy Seafood Aioli.

Spider 10.95
Soft Shell Crab with Avocado, Daikon Sprouts, Masago and Japanese Mayonnaise.

Japanese Bagel 10.50
Salmon, Cream Cheese rolled in Mamenori(Vegetable Seed).

Fusion Rolls

Yum-Yum 11.95
Salmon, Cream Cheese & Asparagus. Flash Fried and Served with Eel Sauce and Lemon Slices.

Lady Dragon 9.95
Tempura Shrimp Roll with Cream Cheese, Avocado & Masago. Topped with Shrimp, Avocado & Eel Sauce.

Fire Dragon 10.50
"Real Crab Meat" Rolled with Avocado, Cucumber & Wrapped in Broiled Eel with a Spicy Eel Sauce.

Lobster Roll 17.00
Butter Poached Lobster Baked on "Real King Crab", Avocado & Cucumber Roll.

Asian Cajun 13.95
Crawfish Aioli with Blackened Snapper Served with Cajun Mayonnaise.

Dragon Roll 12.95
Tempura Shrimp with Cream Cheese & Flying Fish Roe. Topped with BBQ Eel & drizzled with Eel Glaze.

Combinations

Sushi Dinner *(7 pc) Sushi & California Roll* 21.95
Sashimi Dinner *(21 pc) 3 pieces each of 7 types (Chef's Selection)* 29.95
Sashimi Sampler *(9 pc) 3 pieces each of 3 types (Chef's Selection)* 13.95
Sushi & Sashimi Sampler *(7 pc) Sushi, (9 pc) Sashimi & California Roll* 32.95

Side Ways

Seaweed Salad	Edamame	Ika Salad
Traditional Wakame	Soy Bean	Marinated Squid
4.95	5.95	5.95

RED LOBSTER...THE BEGINNING

JOHNNIE'S HIDEAWAY
Lake Buena Vista
Established 2008

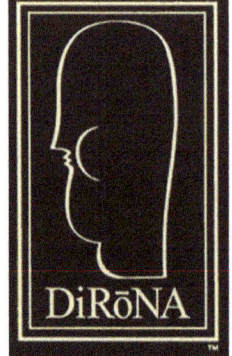

RESTAURANTS

This Week's Dinner Menu

CLARK WOODSBY, Chef Partner   **JAMAL BENSAOUI**, Operating Partner

JOIN US EVERY MONDAY NIGHT FOR ALL-YOU-CAN-EAT FRESH FLORIDA STONE CRAB CLAWS!

Johnnie's Classic Platter ... 39
Stone Crab, Blue Crab, Alaskan King Crab & Crusher Claws

Florida Cracker Platter ... 15.5
fried shrimp, calamari, frog legs, & fried green tomatoes

Stone Crabs

Florida Stone Crabs are day boat caught and hand harvested one claw at a time.
At Johnnie's, we buy only the finest and freshest claws available for your enjoyment.

- Medium Stone Crab (7) 29.95
- Large Stone Crab (5) 48.95
- Select Stone Crab (6) 36.95
- Jumbo Stone Crab (3) .... MKT –limited

Served cold with Johnnie's famous mustard sauce.

— Raw Bar —

- ★ Florida Trio Cocktail ... 14
  lobster, sweet shrimp & lump crab
- Classic Shrimp Cocktail ... 12
- Jumbo Lump Crab Cocktail ... 12
- Alaskan King Crab Cocktail ... 13
- Blue Crab Claw Cocktail ... 9
- Oyster Shooter ... 2.75
- Asian Shooter ... 2.75
- Alaskan Crusher Claws (1) ... 6
- Medium Stone Crab (4) ... 13

Steaks & Chops
U.S.D.A PRIME & CHOICE — AGED 5-6 WEEKS

Bone-In Filet Mignon
17-18oz 35.95

Filet Mignon
10oz 29.95
14oz 32.95

Long Bone Dry Aged Ribeye
28oz 38.95

Aging Process
Our Steaks are dry aged, on the bone, for 15 days following three weeks of wet aging. During this period, the sirloins undergo enzymatic change that intensify flavor, deepen color and tenderize the meat by softening the connective tissue. When broiled at 1,800°, the exterior caramelizes, further intensifying the beefiness of our steaks.

King of the Bone N.Y. Strip
28oz Bone-In 32.95

Johnnie's tableside service
Double-cut N.Y. Strip
48oz for two 64.95
Experience old world elegance with our skilled waiters completing the preparation right at your tableside.

- Truffled Portabella Mushrooms w/ Gorgonzola Fondue 5.00
- Asian-style Wagu Sirloin ginger-soy marinade ... 38.95
- Steakhouse Bacon Extra Thick 2.50 by the slice

... All Steaks and Chops include our reddskin roast-garlic mashed potatoes, our famous house salad and Jeannine's Frenchmaid Bakery breads ...

| 9oz Lobster Tail (with entrée only) 16.95 | Butter-Poached Maine Lobster Claw Oscar 7.95 | Gorgonzola Butter Port Wine Glaze 6.95 | Stone Crab Oscar 8.95 | 1-lb. Medium Stone Crab (with entrée only) 19.95 |

— Appetizers —

- Crispy Calamari ... 7
- Pan-fried Frog Legs ... 6.5
- Steamed Penn Cove Mussels ... 11
- Crab Cake ... 12.5
- Crispy Gulf Oysters ... 11
- Truffled Portabella Fries ... 9
- Escargot ... 7
- Tuna Nachos ... 12
- Seared Tuna Sashimi ... 14.5
- Macadamia Shrimp ... 9.5
- Shrimp & Lobster Fritters ... 6
- Char-broiled Garlic Mussels ... 11
- Steamed Clams (One Pound) ... 7.5
- Crispy Blue Fingers ... 7
- Crabmeat Au Gratin ... 10
- Beef Tenderloin Carpaccio ... 14.5

Johnnie's Classics

- Cast Iron Chicken 16
  pressed & roasted until crispy
- Sautéed Calf's Liver 15
  with caramelized onions and steakhouse apple-wood smoked bacon
- Long Bone Veal Margherita 21
  with tomato sauce and provolone
- Cedar Plank Roasted North Atlantic King Salmon ... 23
- Chop't Steak (One Pound - while they last) 18
  Served with choice of grilled onions and green peppers or sautéed mushrooms and mozzarella.
- Long Bone All-Natural Duroc Pork Chop (2" Thick) ... 19

Shrimp - Crab - Lobster

- Giant Madagascar Shrimp De Johnnie's 28
  pan sautéed only the way Johnnie would do it.
- Jumbo Gulf Fried Shrimp - *hand breaded when the ticket enters the kitchen* (add $12 - all you can eat) 19
- Fried Oysters (Apalachicola selects) 18
  served with Florida Key lime tartar sauce and classic cocktail sauce.
- Mixed Grill 29
  Two select fish of the day (chef's choice) served with our shrimp and scallop scampi.
- Fried Fisherman's Feast (add Macadamia Fried Lobster $9.95) 28
  shrimp, shrimp & lobster fritters, scallops, grouper fingers, and frog legs.
- Dayboat Jumbo Scallops 21
  pan sautéed, pan roast or french fried.
- Alaskan King Crab (1½ Pound) 31
- Blue Crab Stuffed Maine Lobster 36
- Broiled Florida Lobster Tail (1 to 1-1/4 pound) 49
  Tender lobster tail delicately prepared with seasoned bread crumbs and fresh drawn butter, then baked to perfection. (larger tails add 2.75 per oz - Ask server for available sizes)

All Entrees include our famous house salad and Jeannine's Frenchmaid Bakery breads

Potatoes, Vegetables & Sides
Large Enough to Share

Buttermilk French Fried Onions 5.95			Cajun Breaded Mushrooms 6.95
Creamy Spinach 5.95	Wild Mushrooms Sauté 6.95	French Fried Sweet Potato 5.95	Sea-salt Baked Potato loaded tableside 5.95
Fully-loaded "Big Boy" Tater-Tots 6.95	Asparagus with hollandaise & provolone 8.95	Deep Dish Hash Browns 8.95	French Cut Green Beans smoky almonds & brown butter 5.95
Lobster Mac & Cheese 7.95	French Fries 5.95	Fried Green Tomatoes 6.95	Redskin Roast-Garlic Mash 4.95

Consuming raw or undercooked meats, poultry, seafood, shellfish, or eggs may increase your risk of food-borne illness, especially if you have a medical condition.

— Soup & Salad —

- Stone Crab Bisque ... 9
- Cedar Key Clam Chowder ... 7.5
- B.L.T. Salad ... 6
  applewood smoked bacon, iceberg, and Heirloom tomatoes.
- Tuscan Caesar ... 6
  add white Spanish anchovies ... 2
- Baby Iceberg Wedge ... 6
  applewood smoked bacon, tomato, and Point Reyes buttermilk bleu cheese ranch
- Johnnie's Famous House Salad ... 3.5
  served a la carte with asiago bread

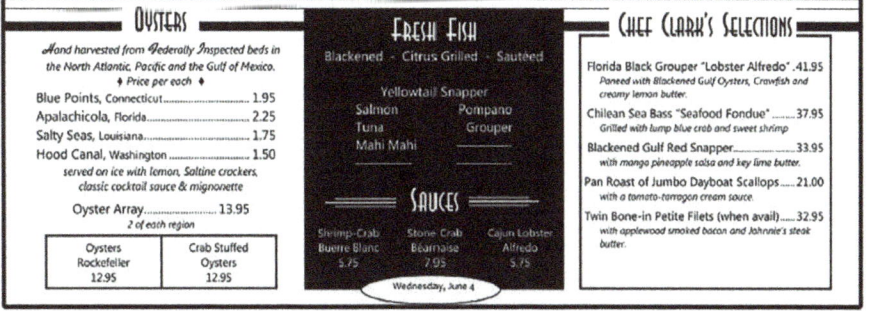

Oysters

Hand harvested from Federally Inspected beds in the North Atlantic, Pacific and the Gulf of Mexico.
♦ *Price per each* ♦

- Blue Points, Connecticut 1.95
- Apalachicola, Florida 2.25
- Salty Seas, Louisiana 1.75
- Hood Canal, Washington 1.50

served on ice with lemon, Saltine crackers, classic cocktail sauce & mignonette

Oyster Array 13.95
2 of each region

| Oysters Rockefeller 12.95 | Crab Stuffed Oysters 12.95 |

Fresh Fish
Blackened · Citrus Grilled · Sautéed

Yellowtail Snapper
Salmon   Pompano
Tuna   Grouper
Mahi Mahi

Sauces

| Shrimp-Crab Buerre Blanc 5.75 | Stone Crab Béarnaise 7.95 | Cajun Lobster Alfredo 5.75 |

Wednesday, June 4

Chef Clark's Selections

- Florida Black Grouper "Lobster Alfredo" .41.95
  Paneed with Blackened Gulf Oysters, Crawfish and creamy lemon butter.
- Chilean Sea Bass "Seafood Fondue" 37.95
  Grilled with lump blue crab and sweet shrimp
- Blackened Gulf Red Snapper 33.95
  with mango pineapple salsa and key lime butter.
- Pan Roast of Jumbo Dayboat Scallops 21.00
  with a tomato-tarragon cream sauce.
- Twin Bone-in Petite Filets (when avail) ... 32.95
  with applewood smoked bacon and Johnnie's steak butter.

RED LOBSTER...THE BEGINNING

The Talk of the Town Restaurant Group is the corporate name for the Woodsby family's restaurants. This locally grown, nationally known restaurant group has been recognized with awards—including the Golden Palm Restaurant Award, the Beef Backer Award, the Award of Excellence, and the Best of Award of Excellence in *Wine Spectator* magazine—every year since 1995. Other awards include Sante Restaurants awards, the *Wine Enthusiast* magazine Award of Distinction, Zagat Survey, and the International Restaurant & Hospitality Diamond Wind Award of Excellence. Charley's Steak House has received the Achievement of Excellence Award from the American Culinary Federation. Charley's Steak House has also been on America's top-ten steak house list every year since 1995. It has held the number-one spot in the country since 2007. All the Charley's Steak Houses, as well as the Italian concept Vito's Chop House, have received the Distinguished Restaurants of North America (DiRoNA) Award of Excellence. FishBones has made the top-ten seafood list since the list's inception in 2001 and was awarded the DiRoNA in 2008. FishBones was inducted into the Seafood Hall of Fame in 2006. Another concept, MoonFish, was named to the top-ten seafood list in 2006, and it was also awarded the DiRoNA the same year. The Woodsbys' most recent restaurant, Johnnie's Hideaway, is also a recipient of the coveted DiRoNA award. More recently all the Talk of the Town restaurants have been recognized with awards such as Expedia Local Expert's Best Restaurant Brand, OpenTable's Diners' Choice Award, and TripAdvisor's Award of Excellence.

AWARDS

With my son Ron, accepting the award from Distinguished Restaurants of North America

2006 Lifetime Achievement Award from the Florida Restaurant & Lodging Association

The Lifetime Achievement Award is presented to those individuals who have "distinguished themselves in an extraordinary manner during their careers" not only in the industry but also in community involvement.

RED LOBSTER...THE BEGINNING

JEB BUSH
GOVERNOR OF THE STATE OF FLORIDA

September 9, 2006

Dear Friends:

It is my pleasure to recognize Charley Woodsby, co-founder of Red Lobster and Talk of the Town Restaurants, on receiving the 2006 Florida Restaurant and Lodging Association's Lifetime Achievement Award.

Charley Woodsby entered the restaurant industry at eighteen and at the age of 38 co-founded the family friendly seafood chain - Red Lobster. Mr. Woodsby's love for the restaurant business has continued and today his namesake restaurant, Charley's Steakhouse, is ranked among the best steakhouses in America.

As philanthropists, Mr. and Mrs. Woodsby have selflessly focused their efforts on helping children develop their full potential. In addition to many educational ventures, Mr. Woodsby is responsible for the building of four churches in Honduras, providing those communities with a place to worship and learn.

Best wishes for continued success.

Sincerely,

Jeb Bush

JB/cas/lnm

Florida Restaurant and Lodging Association

AWARDS

OFFICE OF
BUDDY DYER
MAYOR

October 27, 2006

Charley Woodsby
Talk of the Town Restaurants, Inc.
1260 Central Florida Pkwy
Orlando, FL 32837

Dear Mr. Woodsby:

Let me take this opportunity to congratulate you receiving The Florida Restaurant and Lodging Associations, Lifetime Achievement Award. This is a great honor.

The City of Orlando is proud of our strong business leaders and dedicated professionals. Thank you for being an active part of our community and for making Central Florida your home.

Once again, congratulations on your achievements and good luck to you in the future.

Sincerely,

Buddy Dyer
Mayor

ORLANDO CITY HALL • 400 SOUTH ORANGE AVENUE • P.O. BOX 4990 • ORLANDO, FLORIDA 32802-4990
PHONE 407-246-2221 • FAX 407-246-2842 • WEB SITE WWW.CITYOFORLANDO.NET

With Talk of the Town corporate chef Dan Drayer, CEC—Orlando Escoffier Dinner on July 18, 2012, at Charley's Steak House, International Drive

This was the first dinner in Orlando of the nation's foremost fraternity of dedicated gastronomes, Les Amis d'Escoffier Society. The society gets its name from Auguste Escoffier, "the Chef of Kings and the King of Chefs." The goal is to support culinary education through scholarships to student chefs and to provide support for students pursuing a career in the hospitality industry. The purple medal is the Escoffier Medal of Merit, one of the highest medals awarded.

AWARDS

Chef Pete Harrison, Chef Brian Fry, Chef Dan Drayer, Senior Operating Partner Seth Miller, Chef Clark Woodsby, Paul Darmoc: James Beard House, New York, New York, September 22, 2012

James Beard was a strong driving force of American cuisine and helped educate and mentor generations of professional chefs and food enthusiasts. The Beard Foundation continues to educate our culinary culture. The James Beard House is New York's best-kept gastronomic secret because they showcase the country's top culinary artists.

RED LOBSTER...THE BEGINNING

**James Beard Foundation Dinner
Featuring Talk of the Town Restaurant Group**

Reception ~ SCHUG 2009 Rouge de Noirs Brut (Sparkling Pinot Noir)
Champagne Poached Connecticut Blue Point Oysters with
Roma Tomato and Italian Parsley
Hawaiian Yellow Fin "Ahi" Tuna Tartare with Roast Sweet Pepper Rouille
and Sun Dried Tomato Oil
Crispy Portobello Mushrooms with North Country Apple
Smoked Bacon-Gorgonzola Fondue and Crispy Herbs

1st Course ~ SCHUG 2010 Chardonnay, Sonoma Coast
Lobster Bisque En Croute with Butter-Poached Nova Scotia Lobster,
Fresh Tarragon, and Dry Sack Sherry

2nd Course ~ SCHUG 2011 Sauvignon Blanc, Sonoma Coast
Cedar Plank Roasted Blue Jumbo Lump Crab Cake with Madras Curry,
Sweet Peppers, and Pineapple Mango Salsa "Cream"

3rd Course ~ SCHUG 2009 Pinot Noir, Sonoma Coast
Wasabi-Mirin Chilean Sea Bass with Alaskan Red King Crab Crust,
King Crab Salad, and Wasabi Beurre Blanc

4th Course ~ SCHUG 2009 Pinot Noir, Carneros
Butter Poached "Florida" Lobster-Sea Scallop Medallion
with Homemade Teriyaki-White Truffle Cream

Entrée ~ SCHUG 2007 Merlot, Carneros "Heritage Reserve"
BBQ Prime Harris Ranch Angus Fillet with Wood Roasted Brown Butter Chanterelles,
Horseradish Crème Fraiche, and Rosemary Steak Butter–Au Jus

Dessert ~ SCHUG 2008 Chardonnay, Carneros
McIntosh Apple "Tart" with Warm Salted Caramel,
Candied Pecans, and Cinnamon Cream

AWARDS

AMERICAN WAY | NEXOS CELEBRATED LIVING

Dining

The Platinum List 2016

Photo by Elizabeth Lavin

BEST RESTAURANTS

Charley's Steak House
Tampa, Florida
This award-winning restaurant knows how to flame-grill a steak, and does so over a 1,200-degree citrus- and oak-burning pit. Take time to peruse the impressive wine list, which features more than 800 options. *Charleyssteakhouse.com*

The Lighthouse Club Award was presented in 2016 honoring me as cofounder of Red Lobster Restaurants

AWARDS

WOODSBY FAMILY MEMORIES

With Jean, 1965

Fishing off the Bahamas in my Hatteras

Dirt bike riding in the '70s

Ron in his dune buggy, 1974

RED LOBSTER...THE BEGINNING

Harris, Clark, Dana, me, Jean, and Ron

Jean showing off her new apron

With Jean in Hawaii

Me and Jean

Cutting my favorite stuffed pork crown roast, Christmas, 1990

With Dan Quayle

My children: Ron, Sherry, and Debbie

MaryLou and I were married in 2007

Sherry's Family

Nicole, Sherry, Bill, and Josh

Nicole and Bentley

Ron's Family

Ron and Dana

Clark and Emily with Cora

Sarah with Jimmy, Harris, and Belle

Debbie's Family

Debbie and John

Jay with Jayce and Shannon

Madison, Keith, Alex, Jennifer, and Tanner

Aidan and JT

Grandson JT, is following in his grandfather's footsteps and is owner/operator of two Pita Pits in Columbia, South Carolina

RED LOBSTER...THE BEGINNING

Grandson E. Clark Woodsby, executive chef

Grandson Harris Woodsby and Matt Fellows with their 565-pound trophy alligator measuring 12 feet 6 inches, which they caught September 12, 2013, on the Kissimmee River below the locks at State Road 60

Three generations of the Woodsby family

WOODSBY FAMILY MEMORIES

MaryLou's Family

Sean with Brooklyn, Kristin, me, Beckett, MaryLou, Dylan, Nate, and Jennifer

Sean and Kristin with Brooklyn

Dylan, Jennifer with Hendrix, Nate, and Beckett

MaryLou and me with our Honduran children in 2007

One of the churches in Honduras that Jean and I built

My family birthday in 2008: Bill, Clark, Sherry, JT, Ron, Dana, Harris, Jennifer, Alex, Nicole, Shannon, Debbie, John, MaryLou, me, and Josh

With MaryLou in Athens, Greece, in 2011

Dinner in Lake Bellagio, Italy, in 2014

With MaryLou in Tiananmen Square, China, in 2012

RED LOBSTER...THE BEGINNING

Family trip to Israel in 2014: (top) Sean, me, Brother Jim, Keith, and Nate; (bottom) Kristin, Nicole, Shannon, Debbie, MaryLou, Jennifer S., and Jennifer L.

Our children and spouses at my eighty-fifth birthday: Nate, Jennifer, Sean, Kristin, MaryLou, me, Ron, Dana, Debbie, Bill, and Sherry

RECIPES

In the following pages, you'll find some of the best recipes from our restaurants through the years. Enjoy!

RED LOBSTER...THE BEGINNING

THE THUNDERBIRD INN

Broiled Lobster Tails

Ingredients:

* Lobster tails
* Unsalted butter
* Seasoned salt
* Fresh-ground black pepper

Preparation:

1. Preheat the broiler, and place the oven rack at the second-highest position.
2. Use a pair of kitchen shears to cut a slit up the center of each lobster shell. Do not cut the meat.
3. Carefully open the shells along the midline.
4. When the opening is large enough, gently separate the lobster meat from the inside of the shell with your fingers. Lift it up and out of the opening so that it is sitting on top of the shell.
5. Brush the lobster meat lightly with melted butter, and sprinkle some seasoned salt.
6. Place under the broiler, and cook until the meat is opaque and cooked through. Serve immediately with fresh lemon wedges and the melted butter.

RECIPES

Slow-Roasted Perfect Prime Rib

Ingredients:

* Aged choice prime rib roast, 21–23 pounds
* 4 tablespoons freshly ground pepper
* 8 tablespoons coarse salt
* 2 yellow onions, chopped
* 1½ cups dry red wine

Preparation:

1. Heat oven to 450 degrees. Rub prime rib all over with salt and pepper. Transfer to a heavy metal roasting pan. Arrange fat side up. Cook 20 minutes.

2. Reduce oven to 325 degrees and cook until roast reaches 115 degrees, about 1 hour and 25 minutes. If it hasn't, return to oven; check temperature at 10-minute intervals.

3. Transfer roast to platter; set aside in warm spot for juices to collect. (As roast rests, temperature will increase about 10 degrees.) Do not tent or the crust will get soggy. Adjust oven to 425 degrees.

4. Drain off excess fat. Place pan on top of stove, add onions, and cook and stir over medium heat 3–5 minutes. Deglaze pan with red wine; add beef broth, and scrape up crispy bits and meat juices attached to pan. Simmer until rich and delicious. Strain and keep warm.

5. Creamed horseradish sauce, a simple sauce made with unsweetened whipped heavy cream, ground horseradish, and a pinch of salt, is a traditional and yummy accompaniment for prime rib.

Lobster Cocktail with Continental Sauce

Ingredients:

- ½ gallon water
- 1 onion, chopped
- 1 lemon, sliced
- 3 bay leaves
- 6 whole black peppercorns
- ½ tablespoon salt
- 2 whole lobsters

Dressing:

- ½ cup mayonnaise
- 3 tablespoons ketchup
- 1 tablespoon brandy

Preparation:

1. Fill a large pot with water, and mix in the onion, lemon, bay leaves, peppercorns, and salt. Bring to a boil.
2. Place live lobsters in the boiling water, and cook until bright red, about 12 minutes for 1 pound and about 5 more minutes for each additional pound.
3. Remove the cooked lobsters from the pot, and rinse under cold water. Chill in the refrigerator, and serve cold.
4. In a small bowl, mix the mayonnaise, ketchup, and brandy. Serve as a dipping sauce with the lobster.

Meatloaf

Ingredients:

- 6 ounces garlic-flavored croutons
- ½ teaspoon ground black pepper
- ½ teaspoon cayenne pepper
- 1 teaspoon chili powder
- 1 teaspoon dried thyme
- ½ onion, medium chop
- 1 carrot, peeled and broken
- 3 whole cloves garlic
- ½ red bell pepper
- 36 ounces ground chuck
- 1½ teaspoon kosher salt
- 1 egg

Glaze:

- ½ cup ketchup
- 1 tablespoon honey
- Worcestershire sauce
- Hot pepper sauce

Preparation:

1. Heat the oven to 325 degrees. In a food processor bowl, combine croutons, black pepper, cayenne pepper, chili powder, and thyme. Pulse until the mixture is of a fine texture. Place this mixture into a large bowl.
2. Combine the onion, carrot, garlic, and red pepper in the food processor bowl. Pulse until the mixture is finely chopped but not pureed.
3. Combine the vegetable mixture, ground sirloin, and ground chuck with the bread-crumb mixture. Season the meat mixture with the kosher salt. Add the egg and combine thoroughly, but avoid squeezing the meat.
4. Pack this mixture into a 10-inch loaf pan.
5. Combine the ketchup, Worcestershire, hot pepper sauce, and honey. Brush the glaze onto the meatloaf when it is halfway done and again just before removing from oven.

Southern Golden-Brown Pan-Fried Chicken

Ingredients:

* 1 broiler/fryer chicken, cut into 8 pieces
* 2 cups buttermilk
* 2 tablespoons kosher salt
* 2 tablespoons paprika
* 2 teaspoons garlic powder
* ½ teaspoon cayenne pepper
* Flour for dredging
* Vegetable shortening for frying

Preparation:

1. Cut chicken into 8 pieces, place into a plastic container, and cover with buttermilk. Cover and refrigerate for 12–24 hours.
2. Melt enough shortening to come about one-third of the way up the side of a cast-iron skillet, and heat to 325 degrees.
3. Drain chicken in a colander. Combine salt, paprika, garlic powder, and cayenne pepper. Liberally season chicken with this mixture. Place chicken in flour, let rest until thoroughly coated (about 10 minutes), and gently shake off excess.
4. Place chicken skin side down into the pan. Put thighs in the center and breast and legs around the edge of the pan. The oil should come halfway up the pan.
5. Cook chicken until golden brown on each side, approximately 12–14 minutes per side.
6. Drain chicken and serve hot and crispy.

Pan-Fried Spring Chicken Livers with Crispy Bacon on Toast

Ingredients:

- Canola oil
- 1 pound chicken livers, trimmed
- 1 cup buttermilk
- 2 cups self-rising flour
- 1 tablespoon kosher salt
- 1 tablespoon garlic powder
- 2 teaspoons freshly ground black pepper
- Crispy bacon
- Toast

Preparation:

1. Pour oil in large, deep cast-iron skillet or 4-quart saucepan to reach depth of 2 inches. Heat oil over medium-high heat until deep-fry thermometer registers 340 degrees.
2. Soak livers in buttermilk for 5 minutes.
3. Combine flour, salt, and pepper in a small baking dish.
4. Drain livers, dredge in flour mixture, shake off excess flour, and transfer to a plate.
5. Heat the oil in a skillet. When the oil is quite hot (drops of water will bounce when flicked into the pan), arrange the livers in the skillet so that they are not touching one another.
6. Cover the pan of oil with a frying screen to avoid getting burned by spatters of oil that will pop out as the livers fry. Deep fry the livers until crisp and golden brown, 5–6 minutes. Transfer livers to a paper-towel-lined plate.
7. Serve on freshly toasted white bread with warm, crispy bacon. This is great with hot sauce.

OLD SOUTH

Beef Stew with Fresh Vegetables

Ingredients:

* 2 pounds stew beef
* 2 tablespoons vegetable oil
* 2 cups beef broth
* 1 tablespoon Worcestershire sauce
* 1 clove garlic, peeled
* 1 or 2 bay leaves
* 1 medium onion, sliced
* 1 teaspoon salt
* 1 teaspoon sugar
* ½ teaspoon pepper
* ½ teaspoon paprika
* 3 large carrots, sliced
* 3 ribs celery, chopped
* 2 tablespoons water
* 2 tablespoons cornstarch

Preparation:

1. Brown the meat in hot oil.
2. Add beef broth, Worcestershire sauce, garlic, bay leaves, onion, salt, sugar, pepper, and paprika.
3. Cover and simmer 1½ hours.
4. Remove bay leaves and garlic clove. Add carrots and celery.
5. Cover and cook 30–40 minutes longer.
6. Combine water and cornstarch, and stir until smooth. Add to thicken gravy. Stir and cook until bubbly.

Grilled Genuine Calf's Liver with Bacon Strip

Ingredients:

- 12 ounces bacon, sliced
- 10 tablespoons (1 stick plus 2 tablespoons) unsalted butter, cold
- 6 tablespoons chopped onions
- ½ teaspoon salt
- 6 eight-ounce slices calf's liver, cut into ½-inch slices
- Salt and freshly ground black pepper to taste
- 1 tablespoon unsalted butter
- Sautéed onions (recipe follows)

Sautéed onions:

- 6 tablespoons (¾ stick) unsalted butter
- 3 small onions, thinly sliced
- ½ teaspoon salt
- Melt butter in a large skillet over high heat. Reduce heat.
- Sauté onions with salt, stirring occasionally, until golden brown, about 15 minutes.

Preparation:

1. Fry bacon until crisp. Drain on paper towels and set aside.
2. Melt 4 tablespoons butter in a medium skillet over moderate heat. Cook onions with salt until soft and nearly golden, about 3 minutes.
3. Add cooked bacon, stirring briefly to rewarm.
4. Preheat grill. Season liver with salt and pepper.
5. Grill in melted butter over high heat, about 3 minutes per side.
6. Arrange liver over a bed of sautéed onions, and spoon on sauce.

Country-Fried Flounder

Ingredients:

- 2 pounds flounder fillets, fresh
- 1 cup flour
- ½ teaspoon salt
- ½ teaspoon ground black pepper

Preparation:

1. Skin fillets and cut them into serving-size portions.
2. Combine flour with seasonings. Roll fish in mixture.

Panfry:

1. Place flounder in an iron skillet that has been preheated with about ⅛ inch of oil.
2. Brown on one side for 2–3 minutes.
3. Carefully turn and cook on the other side an additional 3 minutes, until fish flakes easily with a fork.
4. Serve with tartar sauce and coleslaw.

Broiled Whole Flounder

Ingredients:

* 6 tablespoons butter
* 2 teaspoons fresh parsley, finely chopped
* 4 teaspoons fresh lemon juice
* 1/8 teaspoon salt
* 1 small- to medium-size flounder, cleaned and left whole
* Salt and freshly ground pepper

Preparation:

1. Preheat the broiler and broiling pan for 10 minutes.
2. Melt the butter in a heavy saucepan over low heat. Turn off the heat, add the next three ingredients, and mix well.
3. Remove the broiling pan from the oven, and brush the rack with some of the butter sauce.
4. Rinse the cleaned whole flounder, and dry with paper towels. Score the thick top side with four X-shaped slits; season with salt and pepper.
5. Place the fish on the rack and pour about 2 tablespoons of the butter sauce over it. Broil the fish 5–6 minutes at a distance of 3–4 inches from heat.
6. Remove from oven; check for doneness. If the meat flakes easily, it's done. Place on platter, top with remaining butter, and serve with lemon and parsley.
7. Be careful to not overcook the seafood. If overcooked, it becomes dry, and the flavor is depleted.

Place fish close enough to the heat so it can get crispy and browned on the edges. My favorite with a little fresh lemon!

Milk-Fed Veal Cutlet with Tomato Sauce

Ingredients:

- 4 veal cutlets (about 1 pound)
- Salt and pepper
- ½ cup all-purpose flour
- 8 ounces sliced mozzarella cheese
- 1 cup dry seasoned bread crumbs
- 2 eggs, beaten
- Olive oil for frying
- 1 eight-ounce can tomato sauce
- ¼ teaspoon dried basil

Preparation:

1. Sprinkle cutlets with salt and pepper; lightly dredge in flour.
2. Dip cutlets in beaten egg and then seasoned bread crumbs.
3. Heat oil over medium heat. Place breaded cutlets into hot pan. Fry for about 4 minutes on each side or until browned.
4. Place cutlets in baking dish; top with tomato sauce, basil, and mozzarella slices. Bake at 350 degrees for 10–15 minutes.

Great with a little Parmesan cheese, spaghetti, and baked crispy garlic bread.

Broiled Spanish Mackerel

Ingredients:

- 6 three-ounce fillets
- ¼ cup olive oil
- ½ teaspoon paprika
- Salt and ground black pepper to taste
- 12 slices lemon

Preparation:

1. Preheat the oven's broiler, and set the oven rack about 6 inches from the heat source.
2. Lightly grease a baking dish.
3. Rub both sides of each mackerel fillet with olive oil, and place skin side down into the prepared baking dish.
4. Season each fillet with paprika, salt, and pepper.
5. Top each fillet with two lemon slices.
6. Bake the fillets under the broiler until the fish just begins to flake, 5–7 minutes.
7. Serve immediately.

Carrot Raisin Salad

Ingredients:

* 1 pound carrots, peeled and grated
* ½ cup raisins
* 1 cup crushed pineapple
* 1 tablespoon sugar, granulated
* 1 teaspoon grated onion
* ¼ cup mayonnaise
* 1 lemon, juiced
* ½ teaspoon salt
* ¼ teaspoon black pepper
* Lettuce

Preparation:

1. Combine carrots, raisins, pineapple, and sugar in a bowl.
2. Add grated onion, and moisten thoroughly with mayonnaise.
3. Season with lemon, salt, and pepper.
4. Serve on lettuce.

RECIPES

Mashed Potatoes

Ingredients:

* 2 pounds of russet potatoes
* 1 teaspoon salt
* 1 cup half-and-half (half milk and half cream)
* 6 tablespoons butter
* Salt and pepper to taste

Preparation:

1. Peel and quarter the potatoes.
2. Add the potatoes to a large pot with enough cold water to cover them by an inch or so.
3. Add salt and bring the water to a boil.
4. Cook until the potatoes are tender when pierced with a fork.
5. Drain the potatoes, return them to the pot, and cook the drained potatoes over low heat for a couple of minutes to evaporate some of the water still in the potatoes.
6. Mash with potato masher.
7. Blend in butter and half-and-half.
8. Season with salt and pepper.

Southern Smothered Pork Chops and Mashed Potatoes

Ingredients:

* 9 thin-sliced pork chops, center cut
* 1 cup sliced onion, white or yellow
* 1½ cups flour
* 1½ teaspoon salt
* ¼ teaspoon black pepper
* 1 teaspoon garlic powder
* Oil (canola) for browning
* 2 teaspoons margarine
* 2 cups milk

Preparation:

1. Mix together the flour, salt, garlic powder, and pepper. Reserve ½ cup of the seasoned flour and set aside.
2. Rinse the pork chops in cold water and dredge into the 1 cup of seasoned flour.
3. Add oil to a skillet on medium heat. When hot, brown the pork chops in batches, making sure not to crowd the pan. Set browned pork chops to the side.
4. To the hot skillet, add the onions and cook until soft.
5. Add reserved ½ cup of seasoned flour to the soft onions and stir until combined.
6. Whisk milk and margarine into the pan until combined. Bring to a gentle simmer.
7. Add browned pork chops back to the pan and simmer, covered, with the onions for 5–10 minutes until pork chops are tender and sauce has thickened.
8. Serve immediately on top of mashed potatoes.

Fried Fantail Shrimp

Ingredients:

- 1½ pounds large shrimp
- 2 cups milk
- 1 egg
- Seasoned flour
- Cracker crumbs
- ⅛ teaspoon salt
- Dash pepper

Preparation:

1. Mix milk with egg.
2. Mix flour with salt and pepper.
3. Coat shrimp well with flour mixture. Dip shrimp in egg wash, press in cracker breading.
4. Cook shrimp in hot deep fat at 375 degrees until golden brown. Drain on paper towels.

Deviled Crab

Ingredients:

Vegetable Mix:

* 1 pound oleo
* 4 pounds green bell peppers
* 4 pounds celery
* 10 pounds onion

Crab mix:

* 1 ounce Accent flavor enhancer
* 2 dozen eggs
* 1 gallon mayonnaise
* ½ gallon prepared mustard
* 6 ounces Worcestershire sauce
* 1 ounce Tabasco
* 1 ounce salt
* 5 pounds crushed saltines
* 24 pounds claw crabmeat

Preparation:

1. Chop vegetables until fine.
2. Heat oleo; add green bell peppers, celery, and onion. Sauté until tender.
3. Add Accent, eggs, mayonnaise, mustard, Worcestershire, Tabasco, salt, and crushed saltines.
4. Cook over medium heat for about 5 minutes.
5. Cool thoroughly.
6. Add crab, folding in carefully, and adjust seasoning.

RECIPES

GARY'S DUCK INN

Hush Puppy Recipe

Ingredients:

- 2 cups enriched white cornmeal
- ⅓ cup flour
- 2 teaspoons baking powder
- ⅔ cup ground Spanish onion and juice
- 2 tablespoons melted butter
- 1 egg
- ⅔ cup milk (more or less if needed, according to onion juice)

Preparation:

1. Sift meal, flour, baking powder, and salt together.
2. Add butter, onion, and juice to dry ingredients.
3. Add beaten egg. Add enough milk to make a soft dough.
4. Drop by spoonfuls into deep fat at 375 or 400 degrees for about 4–5 minutes.

Originally, Gary's made hush puppies the old-fashioned way, with a spoon. I found a hush puppy wheel at a fish camp in South Carolina. This made them lighter and better than ever.

Seafood Bisque

Ingredients:

- ½ cup flour
- ½ cup butter, melted
- 1 quart milk
- 1 teaspoon garlic powder
- 1 teaspoon salt
- ½ teaspoon white pepper (increase to 1 teaspoon if desired)
- 2 tablespoons butter
- ½ cup sherry
- ½ pound scallops, chopped
- ½ pound shrimp, chopped
- ½ pound crab claw meat, chopped
- 2 teaspoons Accent (optional)

Preparation:

1. Combine flour and melted butter to make a roux.
2. To make cream sauce, put milk in the top of a double boiler. Add garlic powder, salt, and white pepper.
3. When milk is hot, add the roux mixture, and stir to blend.
4. Cover and cook on medium heat until mixture thickens.
5. Melt 2 tablespoons butter with sherry in a sauté pan.
6. Add chopped seafood, and sauté 2 minutes.
7. Add seafood to cream sauce in double boiler. Turn off heat, and let stand for 30 minutes to allow flavors to meld.
8. Reheat and serve.

Gator Tail with Swamp Sauce

Ingredients:

* 2 pounds alligator meat (Gary's Duck Inn manager Rick Dorman recommends tail meat for this recipe)

Egg Wash:

* 2 eggs, beaten
* 2 cups milk

Breading:

* Self-rising flour
* Black pepper to taste
* Salt to taste
* Granulated garlic to taste
* Peanut oil for deep-frying

Marinade:

* 2 cups salad oil
* ¾ cup red wine vinegar
* 1 teaspoon garlic powder
* ½ teaspoon black pepper
* 1 teaspoon oregano
* Dash of salt

Swamp Sauce:

* 1 cup mayonnaise
* ⅛ cup yellow mustard
* ⅛ cup horseradish
* Dash of Worcestershire sauce
* Dash of Tabasco sauce
* Juice of 1 lemon

Preparation:

1. Remove all fat and sinew from gator meat, tenderize between sheets of wax paper, and pound with mallet to about ½-inch thickness. Cut across grain for more tender pieces into 1-inch squares. Combine all ingredients listed for marinade. Marinate in the refrigerator for 24 hours.

2. At preparation time, remove meat from marinade, dip in egg wash, and then dredge in seasoned flour. Deep fry meat pieces at 350 degrees for about 1 minute. Remove with slotted spoon, and drain on paper towel.

3. Stir together swamp sauce ingredients. Serve on the side for dipping.

Aunt Edna's Shrimp Sauce

(Makes enough sauce to flood a battleship—and you'll want it that way)

Ingredients:

* 24 ounces chili sauce
* 24 ounces ketchup
* 10 ounces Worcestershire sauce
* ½ cup mayonnaise
* 3 ounces fresh horseradish (depending on your taste)

Preparation:

1. Mix well in the blender, and serve with shrimp the way you like it.
2. The shrimp wouldn't have that Strickland touch without Charley's Aunt Edna's special shrimp sauce, a sweet and tangy mixture that perfectly complements crispy fried shrimp.

Jean loved to share fried-shrimp dinners with friends during the summer, at twilight, when it was just cool enough to venture out onto the screened-in porch.

Deep-Fried Frog Legs

Ingredients:

* 5 large frog legs, cleaned
* 1 cup flour
* 1 tablespoon lemon pepper
* 1½ teaspoons garlic salt
* 1 teaspoon black pepper
* 2 eggs, beaten
* Cracker crumbs, finely crushed
* Peanut oil for frying

Preparation:

1. Skin frog legs, wash in cold water, and drain thoroughly.
2. Combine flour, lemon pepper, garlic, salt, and black pepper to mix thoroughly.
3. Shake frog legs in the seasoned flour to coat, dip in beaten egg, and roll in cracker crumbs.
4. Deep fry at 360 degrees until golden brown, about 7–8 minutes.

Cover the frog legs with milk for one hour.
This will make them extra juicy!

Canaveral Bay Scallops en Casserole

Ingredients:

- 1 pound cooked Canaveral scallops
- 3 tablespoons butter
- 1 tablespoon olive oil
- 2 cups light cream or half-and-half
- ¼ cup pale dry sherry
- 2 cups sliced baby mushrooms
- 1 diced shallot
- 1 garlic clove, minced
- ¼ cup chopped fresh parsley
- 1 tablespoon Parmesan, ground
- 1½ cups buttery crackers, coarsely crumbled

Preparation:

1. Lightly sauté mushrooms, shallots, and garlic in olive oil. Add sherry and cream, and reduce until lightly thickened.
2. Melt butter; add crumbled crackers, Parmesan, and parsley. Set aside one half of the stuffing mixture.
3. Add scallop mixture to remaining stuffing in pan. Combine well.
4. Pour into casserole dish, and top with the remaining stuffing.
5. Bake in a preheated 325-degree oven until topping is golden brown.
6. While the casserole is baking, sauté extra scallops to use with lemon as a garnish on top of the cooked casserole.
7. Use the baking dish as the serving dish, and deliver to the table bubbling hot.

RECIPES

Gulf Shrimp en Casserole

Ingredients:

- 1 pound cooked jumbo gulf white shrimp
- 3 tablespoons butter
- 1 tablespoon olive oil
- 2 cups light cream or half-and-half
- ¼ cup pale dry sherry
- 2 cups sliced baby mushrooms
- 1 diced shallot
- 1 minced garlic clove
- ¼ cup chopped fresh parsley
- 1 tablespoon Parmesan, ground
- 1½ cups buttery crackers, coarsely crumbled

Preparation:

1. Lightly sauté mushrooms, shallots, and garlic in olive oil. Add sherry and cream, and reduce until lightly thickened.
2. Melt butter; add crumbled crackers, Parmesan, and parsley. Set aside one half of the stuffing mixture.
3. Add shrimp mixture to remaining stuffing in pan. Combine well.
4. Pour into casserole dish, and top with the remaining stuffing.
5. Bake in a preheated 325-degree oven until topping is golden brown.
6. While the casserole is baking, sauté extra shrimp to use with lemon as a garnish on top of the cooked casserole.
7. Use the baking dish as the serving dish, and deliver to the table bubbling hot.

Flounder en Papillote

Ingredients:

- Four 14×12-inch sheets parchment paper
- ¼ pound fresh mushrooms, sliced
- ¼ cup plus 2 tablespoons butter or margarine, divided
- 3 tablespoons all-purpose seasoned flour
- 1 cup milk
- 2 tablespoons sherry
- ½ teaspoon salt
- ¼ teaspoon paprika
- 4 flounder fillets (about 2 pounds)
- ½ pound medium shrimp, peeled and deveined

Preparation:

1. Heat oven to 450 degrees.
2. Cut parchment paper into four heart shapes; fold sheets in half lengthwise.
3. Sauté mushrooms in 1 tablespoon butter in a small skillet until tender. Set aside.
4. Melt 3 tablespoons butter in a heavy saucepan over low heat; add flour, stirring until smooth. Cook 1 minute, stirring constantly. Gradually add milk, sherry, and seasonings; cook over medium heat, stirring constantly, until mixture is thickened and bubbly. Stir in sautéed mushrooms.
5. Melt remaining butter; open paper heart out flat, and lightly brush surface with butter.
6. Place a flounder fillet on half of each paper heart; top each with one-fourth of the shrimp, and pour mushroom sauce evenly over shrimp. Fold paper edges over to seal securely.
7. Carefully place parchment bags on a baking sheet.
8. Bake at 450 degrees until bags are puffed and lightly browned, about 12–14 minutes. Place on individual serving plates before cutting and opening bags.
9. Garnish with lemon wedges.
10. Serve immediately.

The Duck Inn Special:
Lobster Tail Meat, Shrimp, and Scallops in Lemon Butter Sauce

Ingredients:

* 1 pound lobster meat
* 16 jumbo shrimp, cleaned
* 16 jumbo sea scallops, cleaned
* Salt to taste
* Black pepper to taste
* ¼ cup lemon butter, softened
* 2 tablespoons olive oil
* 1 fresh lemon, halved
* 2 tablespoons finely chopped parsley

Lemon Butter Sauce:

* 1 tablespoon olive oil
* 1 shallot, rough chopped
* ½ cup dry white wine
* 2 tablespoons butter
* 2 teaspoons fresh grated lemon peel
* Juice of one lemon
* 1 tablespoon fresh Italian parsley, finely chopped

Lemon Butter Preparation:

1. Sauté the shallot in the olive oil until it becomes soft, about 1½ minutes.
2. Add the white wine, and bring to a boil. Boil until it is reduced by half.
3. Add the butter to the white wine reduction, and cook over medium-low heat until the butter melts. Remove from heat.
4. Strain the shallot; whisk in the lemon peel, lemon juice, and parsley. Set aside and keep warm until ready to use.

Lobster Preparation:

1. Season lobster, shrimp, and scallops with salt and black pepper. Place on hot grill and cook medium rare for 2–3 minutes per side.
2. At the same time as cooking seafood, make the lemon butter sauce.
3. To serve, arrange lobster, shrimp, and scallops on plate.
4. Drizzle lemon butter sauce over dish.
5. Garnish with fresh lemon and chopped parsley.

Shrimp and Scallop Scampi

Ingredients:

* 10 jumbo shrimp, peeled, deveined, and butterflied
* 10 large sea scallops, cleaned
* ¼ pound butter
* 1 cup bread crumbs
* 1 teaspoon fresh garlic, chopped
* ½ cup dry white wine
* 1 teaspoon fresh lemon juice
* Salt to taste
* Black pepper to taste
* 1 pinch paprika
* 2 tablespoons fresh parsley, chopped

Preparation:

1. Place scallops and shrimp in casserole.
2. Melt butter and lightly sauté garlic just until fragrant. Add wine and lemon juice. Stir. Season butter with salt and pepper to taste.
3. Pour mixture over shrimp and scallops.
4. Sprinkle with bread crumbs, paprika, and parsley.
5. Bake at 350 degrees for 14–16 minutes.

**It is best to allow the wine to reduce slightly before adding the fresh lemon; it gets a much richer flavor.
(We kept the chopped garlic, wine, lemon juice, salt, and pepper all mixed up in a bottle!)**

Coleslaw

Ingredients:

- 4 ounces (⅔ cup) granulated sugar
- Dash of salt
- Pinch of black pepper
- Pinch of celery seed
- 1 ounce (1 teaspoon) prepared mustard
- 2½ ounces cider vinegar
- 13 ounces heavy mayonnaise
- ½ ounce (1 tablespoon) fresh lemon juice
- ¾ pound green cabbage, finely chopped
- ½ large carrot, grated

Preparation:

1. In large bowl, mix together all ingredients except cabbage and grated carrot.
2. Stir in cabbage and carrot, and refrigerate to chill.
3. Mixture will keep well in refrigerator.

Fillet of Flounder with Crabmeat Dressing

Crab Dressing Ingredients:

- 1 pound crabmeat, cleaned
- ½ pound butter
- ½ cup red pepper, diced
- ½ cup green onion diced
- 1 teaspoon fresh garlic, minced

Stuffed Flounder Ingredients:

- 2 ten-ounce flounder fillets
- ½ teaspoon salt
- ½ teaspoon black pepper
- Crab dressing (recipe follows)
- ½ teaspoon paprika
- Vegetable oil
- 1 one-inch slice crab butter (recipe follows)
- Fresh parsley for garnish

Crab Dressing Preparation:

1. Melt butter; add peppers, onions, and seasoning.
2. Sauté until lightly soft, approximately 2 minutes. Add crab, remove from heat, and chill thoroughly.

Stuffed Flounder Preparation:

1. Preheat the oven to 350 degrees.
2. Sprinkle flounder with salt and pepper.
3. Stuff the flounder with the crab mix, and press the sides down to cover the filling. Sprinkle with paprika.
4. Coat a baking dish with oil, place the fish in the dish, and bake for 20 minutes.
5. Turn the oven to broil, and broil for 5 additional minutes. Place butter on top of the grilled fish, and sprinkle fresh parsley on top for added color.

Baked Stuffed Shrimp with Crabmeat Stuffing

Ingredients:

- 3 tablespoons melted butter
- 24 U-12 jumbo shrimp
- 24 one-inch pieces of country bacon

Charley's Crab Dressing Ingredients:

- 1 pound crabmeat, backfin lump
- ½ pound butter
- 1 teaspoon black pepper
- ½ cup red pepper, diced
- ½ cup green onion, diced
- 1 teaspoon garlic, minced

Preparation:

1. Melt butter; add pepper, onions, and seasoning.
2. Sauté peppers until lightly soft, approximately 2 minutes.
3. Add crab, remove from heat, and chill thoroughly.
4. Preheat the oven to 375 degrees.
5. Place shrimp in baking dish, spoon the crabmeat stuffing evenly into each shrimp (about 2 tablespoons), and place stuffed sides up.
6. Place bacon on top of crab, and drizzle with the remaining melted butter.
7. Bake until golden, about 16–18 minutes.

Shrimp Salad Louie

Ingredients:

- 2 cups shrimp, cooked, deveined, and peeled
- Chilled iceberg lettuce leaves
- 2 small heads endive cut in half
- 8 tomato wedges
- 2 hard-boiled eggs
- 20 black olives
- 8 lemon wedges

Gary's Louie Dressing:

- 1 ¼ cups Aunt Edna's shrimp sauce
- 2 tablespoons parsley
- 1 tablespoon Worcestershire sauce
- 1 tablespoon steak sauce

Preparation:

1. Combine all ingredients for Louie dressing. Chill until needed.
2. Arrange lettuce and endive on chilled salad plates.
3. Place shrimp on greens.
4. Garnish with tomato wedges, hard-cooked eggs, olives, and lemon wedges.
5. Spoon Louie dressing over shrimp.

Jumbo Fried Shrimp

Ingredients:

* 1 pound of jumbo shrimp, peeled, deveined, and butterflied; leave tail intact

Egg Wash:

* 1 large egg
* Pint of milk

Saltine Cracker Breading:

* 1½ cups saltine cracker meal
* Salt to taste
* Black pepper to taste

Preparation:

1. Heat a deep fryer with peanut oil to 360 degrees.
2. Beat the egg and milk together.
3. Dip the cleaned shrimp first into the cracker meal and then into the egg and milk mixture; then dredge again in cracker meal.
4. Drop shrimp carefully into hot oil, and fry until golden brown, about 30 seconds.
5. Remove from oil. Drain on paper towels.

Key Lime Pie

Ingredients:

- 6 ounces key lime juice, fresh
- 28 ounces sweetened condensed milk (not evaporated)
- 1 nine-inch graham cracker or chocolate-cookie crust

Preparation:

1. Over medium-high heat, bring lime juice just to a boil. Remove from heat.
2. Refrigerate for 15 minutes, stir into condensed milk, and pour into pie shell.
3. Place in refrigerator.
4. Top with whipped cream and slice of lime.

Alaskan Crabmeat Cocktail

Ingredients:

- 16 ounces Alaskan crabmeat
- ⅔ cup mayonnaise
- 2 teaspoons lemon juice
- 1 tablespoon fresh chopped parsley
- ⅔ cup finely sliced celery

Preparation:

1. Mix mayonnaise, lemon juice, fresh chopped parsley, and seasoning.
2. Add the celery and mix well.
3. Add crabmeat, mix gently, and chill thoroughly.
4. Place romaine leaf on plate, fill with crab salad, and garnish with fresh chopped parsley.

LOBSTER

Broiled Lobster Tails

Preparation:

1. Cut lengthwise down the middle through the top of the lobster tail shell, pinch the tail together, and crack the last shell section free from the meat.

2. Lay the shell open so the meat is exposed, pull the meat from the end of the tail, and lightly score the underside crosswise about 1 inch apart.

3. Return the shell to the closed position, lay the meat on top of the shell, spread the tail, and break the tail muscle with your thumb. This keeps the tail from curling when the lobster is cooked. Score the top of the lobster meat lengthwise down each side and the center, brush with seasoned butter, and sprinkle with your favorite seafood seasoning before cooking.

4. Broil just until the lobster meat is opaque and firm to the touch, about 1 minute per ounce.

Grilled Lobster Tails

Ingredients:

- 1 teaspoon salt
- 1 teaspoon paprika
- ⅛ teaspoon freshly ground pepper
- ⅛ teaspoon garlic powder
- ½ cup oil
- 1 tablespoon fresh lemon juice
- 2 ten-ounce lobster tails

Preparation:

1. Split tails lengthwise with a large knife.
2. Mix seasoning with oil and lemon juice; brush meat side of tail with marinade.
3. Preheat grill, place tails meat side down, and grill until well scored, approximately 5–6 minutes.
4. Turn over lobster and cook just until opaque, about 5 minutes. Brush often with remaining marinade.

Roasted Maine Lobster with Crabmeat Stuffing

Ingredients:

* 1 pound blue crabmeat, cleaned
* 1 teaspoon shallot, minced
* 1 teaspoon parsley, chopped
* 1 tablespoon mayonnaise
* 1 tablespoon coarse bread crumbs
* 1 whole egg
* 1 teaspoon fresh lemon juice
* ⅛ teaspoon Worcestershire sauce
* 2 whole Maine lobsters, 1½ pounds are perfect
* Butter, cut into pieces
* Paprika
* Fresh lemon juice

Preparation:

1. For the stuffing: Blend all stuffing ingredients except crab. Fold in crabmeat.
2. For the lobsters: Split lengthwise, remove stomach sac, and fill with crab stuffing.
3. Crack claws with the blunt side of knife.
4. Pour lemon juice on tail meat, sprinkle with paprika, and dot with pieces of butter.
5. Bake in a 400-degree oven for 15 minutes.
6. Serve with melted butter and lemon wedges.

TALK OF THE TOWN

Cedar-Plank-Roasted Atlantic King Salmon

Ingredients:

- 8 ounces of salmon
- 2 cups good-quality olive oil
- 2 egg yolks
- Juice of 2 lemons
- Pinch of kosher salt
- 2 cups grated Parmesan cheese
- 2 cups red onion, ¼-inch dice

Preparation:

1. Combine the egg and lemon juice; mix in a food processor.
2. Add the oil very slowly until blended. Add remaining ingredients, and blend thoroughly by hand.
3. Place Atlantic king salmon fillet on well-soaked cedar plank, and spread with an even layer of mixture.
4. Place salmon on a preheated grill. Grill over very high heat with lid closed until crust is golden brown.
5. Open lid and cook to medium rare. Total cook time is approximately 10–12 minutes.

Grilled Caesar Salad

Ingredients:

* Romaine lettuce, rinsed and halved
* Olive oil
* Kosher salt
* Freshly ground black pepper
* Your favorite Caesar dressing

Preparation:

1. Arrange romaine halves on a sheet tray.
2. Brush each head of romaine with 1 tablespoon olive oil per side.
3. Season with the kosher salt.
4. Season with freshly ground black pepper
5. Lightly grill romaine halves until very lightly charred.
6. Remove from grill, and chill thoroughly.
7. Quarter the romaine halves.
8. Cut remaining romaine into 1-inch pieces.
9. Toss lightly with your favorite Caesar dressing and croutons.
10. Serve with freshly shaved Parmesan.

Clam Chowder

Ingredients:

* 2 tablespoons butter
* 1 cup diced onion
* ½ cup diced celery
* ½ cup diced leeks
* ¼ teaspoon chopped garlic
* 2 tablespoons flour
* 1 quart milk, hot
* 1 cup clams in juice
* 1 cup diced potatoes
* 1 tablespoon salt
* ¼ teaspoon white pepper
* 1 teaspoon dry thyme
* ½ cup heavy cream

Preparation:

1. In a soup pot, melt butter over medium heat, add onion, celery, leeks, and garlic, and sauté for 3 minutes; stir frequently.
2. Remove from heat and add flour, mixing well. Slowly add milk, and whisk until creamy.
3. Add clam juice, slowly bring just to a boil, mix often, and reduce to a simmer.
4. Add potatoes and seasonings. Finish with heavy cream, add clams, and simmer just to warm through.

Our clam chowder was originally made from scratch, and the volume was so great that we soon had to triple the recipe, storing it in huge containers.

Alaskan King Crab Au Gratin

Ingredients:

- 8 tablespoons butter
- ½ cup yellow onion, small dice
- 2 tablespoons seasoned all-purpose flour
- 1 cup milk, warm
- ½ teaspoon salt
- Ground white pepper to taste, about 1 pinch
- ¼ cup sherry
- 12 ounces Alaskan king crabmeat
- 1 cup finely crumbled crackers
- ½ cup finely grated cheddar cheese
- Grated Parmesan to taste

Preparation:

1. Crumble crackers evenly. Reserve just enough crumbs and cheese for a nice top crust on the casserole.
2. Melt one half of the butter in a large, heavy skillet. Sauté onion just until tender and just lightly browned; slowly add flour until all butter is used.
3. Stir constantly over low heat, and when all flour is blended, gradually add hot milk. Continue stirring over low heat. When the sauce starts to thicken, add salt, pepper, and sherry.
4. Mix crabmeat, sauce, and the extra cracker crumbs and cheese.
5. Place in a lightly greased baking dish.
6. Sprinkle reserved cracker crumbs and cheese on the top of the casserole.
7. Dot with remaining butter, and bake at 350 degrees until the top is golden brown, about 15 minutes.
8. Add additional grated Parmesan cheese, if desired.

RECIPES

Shrimp and Scallop Scampi

Ingredients:

- 1 cup white wine
- ½ cup butter
- 3 teaspoons fresh garlic, minced
- ½ pound shrimp, peeled and deveined
- ½ pound scallops, cleaned
- Salt and pepper
- 6 slices cheese

Preparation:

1. Place in dish, add ingredients, and cover with cheese.
2. Bake in a 350-degree oven for 12–15 minutes until cheese is lightly browned.
3. Be careful not to overcook the shrimp. They are ready when they have turned pink.

Country-Fried Flounder

Ingredients:

- 2 pounds fresh flounder fillets
- Salt and pepper
- 1 cup seasoned cornmeal breading

Preparation:

1. Skin fillets, cut into serving portions, season, roll in cornmeal mix, and place in a preheated iron skillet with ¼ inch of oil.
2. Brown on one side 2 minutes, turn, and cook the other side 1–2 minutes, until fish flakes easily with a fork.
3. Serve with tartar sauce, fresh lemons, and coleslaw.

Fried Soft-Shell Crab

Ingredients:

- 18 live soft-shell crabs
- 1 teaspoon salt
- ¼ teaspoon freshly ground black pepper
- ¼ teaspoon garlic powder
- ¼ teaspoon onion powder
- 2 ounces lemon juice
- 1 cup seasoned flour
- 3 eggs, beaten
- 2 cups plain bread crumbs
- Fresh lemons for garnish

Preparation:

1. Clean crabs, but do not remove top shell.
2. Rinse well in cool water.
3. Place the crabs on a sheet pan, and season with salt, pepper, lemon, garlic powder, and onion powder. Then refrigerate for at least 2 hours.
4. Place flour in one bowl, eggs in another, and bread crumbs in the last.
5. Roll crab in the flour, dip in the eggs, and then coat with the bread crumbs.
6. Preheat oven to 450 degrees.
7. Heat a skillet with about 1 inch of oil.
8. Sauté crab on one side for 4–5 minutes, turn, and continue until crab is crispy.
9. Place browned crabs in oven until ready to eat.
10. Serve with remoulade and fresh lemons.

Deep-Fried Flounder with Hush Puppies

Ingredients:

* 4 flounder fillets
* 1 cup milk
* ⅛ teaspoon salt
* ⅛ teaspoon freshly ground black pepper
* 1 cup seasoned flour
* Vegetable oil for frying

Preparation:

1. Rinse and pat fish dry.
2. In a shallow dish, mix together milk, salt, and pepper.
3. Dip pieces of fish in milk mixture.
4. Heat vegetable oil to 350 degrees. Oil should be about ⅔ deep in pan, enough to cover entire fillet. (Alternatively, you can use a deep fryer.)
5. Roll fish in flour, and place in hot oil.
6. Deep fry fish, turning once, until golden brown.
7. Drain on paper towels, and keep warm.
8. Spoon hush puppies into hot oil, and fry until golden brown.

TIPS FOR CRAB LEGS AND LOBSTER

How to Steam Crab Legs

Preparation:

1. Place frozen crab legs in vegetable steamer or colander over boiling water.
2. Cover tightly, and steam approximately 6 minutes.
3. Brush with melted butter. Season and serve with cocktail sauce.

How to Cook a Maine Lobster

Preparation:

1. The easiest way to cook a live lobster is to boil in lightly salted water, similar in flavor to the sea.
2. Place large pot over high heat, bring to a rapid boil, plunge lobster headfirst into water, return to a boil, and cook until lobster floats to the surface, 8–10 minutes.
3. Remove lobster and allow to cool slightly to finish steaming gently in the shell, about 5–8 minutes, before cracking shell open.
4. Serve with melted butter, lemon wedges, lobster crackers, lobster bibs, and big napkins.

RECIPE FOR LIFE

If you have a dream, you have to give it everything you've got. You have to give it your best effort, and go at it with every fiber of your being.

A NOTE FROM THE AUTHORS

Charley Woodsby

Charley Woodsby has a long tradition in the restaurant industry, with a career spanning over sixty years. He began his career by attending culinary school in New York City, and in 1954, he opened his first restaurant in Atlanta, Georgia. He then moved to Jacksonville and formed a business partnership with Bill Darden that would change the rest of his life. The partnership operated numerous successful restaurants in Florida. In 1968, Charley and Bill opened the first Red Lobster in Lakeland, Florida. After two years the partnership sold all five stores to General Mills. Charley stayed with the company to open seventy-two Red Lobster restaurants across the country. At the age of forty-two, Charley retired. His retirement lasted only a year, and he was back in business with his son, Ron, in 1974. Together they opened several Talk of the Town restaurants, and in 1984 they decided to open a high-end steak house named after its founder: Charley's Steak House. Charley felt that quality, value, and service were the cornerstones for building success. Although he is semiretired, his legacy lives on. In 2006, he received the Florida Restaurant & Lodging Association's Lifetime Achievement Award. Charley has three children, seven grandchildren, and ten great-grandchildren.

Chef Dan Drayer, CEC WCMC

Chef Dan Drayer's cooking career began when he was a young boy of six years old cooking in the kitchen with his grandmother. She taught him a true love of food and the power that it holds over people. As a youngster, Dan would go out to dinner with his grandparents when he visited them in Texas. Dan's grandfather especially enjoyed going out to the finer-dining steak and fresh-seafood houses from the Gulf Coast of Texas to New Orleans. "As I look back to those early childhood memories of dining out," Dan says, "I can now appreciate how Charley Woodsby pioneered the dining industry with his vision of the family-dining concept. Back in those days, it was the local dime-store lunch counter, malt shop, or fine-dining steakhouse. Charley came along and gave us the American family dinner table. He imprinted the way for generations ahead to sit down with their families in a comfortable surrounding that was not only affordable but also enjoyable. Working with Charley Woodsby throughout the years and learning from him has been a true honor for me, not only as a chef but as a human being. Charley is selfless, thoughtful, generous, kind, and a true gentleman. I greatly respect him for all that he has done and continues to do. I am privileged to have coauthored this book about his life and proud to call him my friend."

My goal in life is to help those in need and share the message of the Gospel. Hopefully, I will leave this earth a better place because of what I did and who I was.

Charley

ADDITIONAL PRAISE

"Mr. Woodsby's love for the restaurant business has continued and today his namesake restaurant, Charley's Steakhouse, is ranked among the best steakhouses in America."

—JEB BUSH, FLORIDA GOVERNOR 1999–2007, IN A PERSONAL LETTER RECOGNIZING CHARLEY WOODSBY FOR A LIFETIME ACHIEVEMENT AWARD FROM THE FLORIDA RESTAURANT AND LODGING ASSOCIATION, SEPTEMBER 9, 2006

"What I have most admired about Charley is his attention to detail and his demand for excellence. You can walk into any of his restaurants and immediately know it's one of his. They look and behave exactly as you would want a restaurant to. Like him, they are dignified and understated, but have a wealth of substance. Success did not befall him; he earned it."

—PAUL MEARS, CHAIRMAN, MEARS TRANSPORTATION GROUP

"Charley has been a mentor to me for the past thirty years. His guidance, both professionally and personally, has been invaluable to me and my career. In my opinion, Charley's key to success has been that first he treats everyone with respect and second he sees everyone as a member of his extended family. His longevity in the restaurant business is an inspiration and a testament to his magnitude in the industry."

—DENNIS DARMOC, CFO, TALK OF THE TOWN RESTAURANTS INC.

"At some point in every conversation with Charley, I think to myself, 'I cannot believe I am talking to a man who helped shape the way we dine out.' Charley is an inspiration to me not only professionally but personally. It is an honor to learn from a true industry pioneer."

—SETH MILLER, SENIOR OPERATIONS PARTNER,
TALK OF THE TOWN RESTAURANTS INC.

"To be a great restaurant you need talent from the kitchen to the front of the house and certainly Charley exceeds all those achievements!"

—CHEF BURT CUTINO, CEC, AAC, HOF, HBOT, COFOUNDER OF SARDINE FACTORY RESTAURANT AND PAST CHAIR OF AMERICAN ACADEMY OF CHEFS, 1995–1999

"All that I had done before and the years since, nothing has excited me more than the time working with Charley Woodsby, Bill Darden, Wally Buckley and the dozens of others that contributed to the phenomenon in the early '70s."

—WILLIAM MACK MILLER, EXECUTIVE DIRECTOR WHO STARTED THE ARCHITECTURAL AND GENERAL CONTRACTOR DIVISION AND HANDLED THE RAPID EXPANSION

"Charley Woodsby is a true AMERICAN entrepreneur of the restaurant business which represents one of the hardest industries to be successful. Many of his innovations have changed how restaurants operate. Blessed with an inquisitive mind and huge creative talent, Woodsby is a case study of success."

—JAMES DOHERTY, PUBLISHER AND EDITOR,
NATION'S RESTAURANT NEWS EMERITUS

CPSIA information can be obtained
at www.ICGtesting.com
Printed in the USA
LVHW071649301018
595299LV00040BB/1039/P